Good Housekeeping's
DREAMY DESSERTS

By the
Food Editors
of
Good
Housekeeping
Magazine

ILLUSTRATIONS BY
TYE GIBSON

PHOTOGRAPHS BY
JAMES VILES
AND PAUL DOME

Published by
Consolidated Book Publishers
1727 South Indiana Avenue, Chicago, Illinois 60616

Contents

No meal, we feel, is complete without the dessert (as any member of your family will agree). But how to choose from

Dreamy Desserts

so many delectable recipes? The rule is simple: Keep the rest of the meal in mind when you plan its finale. If the meal is light, a hearty dessert is right. If the weather is hot, a hot dessert is not. Is the meal short on starchy food? Then a pudding or cake-dessert is good. And if it's company you expect—a super, dazzling dessert creation is correct!

Cake-Desserts

APRICOT SPARKLE CAKE
(Pictured opposite)

1 1-pound ½-ounce package
    spongecake mix
½ pound packaged dried apricots
1 3-ounce package orange-flavor
    gelatin

¼ cup granulated sugar
1 tablespoon lemon juice
⅛ teaspoon almond extract
Dessert topping (optional)

Day before:
1. Make and bake spongecake from mix as package label directs, using ungreased 10-inch tube pan; cool as directed. Brush loose crumbs from top and sides of cake; wrap in saran; refrigerate overnight.
2. In 1½-quart saucepan pour 3 cups water over apricots; bring to boil, then simmer about 45 minutes, or until apricots are tender.
3. Remove 7 apricot halves for garnish; set aside to cool. Reserve liquid from remaining apricots; then purée these apricots by forcing through a fine sieve. Now add enough reserved apricot liquid to make 2 cups pulp and juice. Cover; refrigerate overnight, along with apricot halves.

Early on day, or at least 3 hours before serving:
1. In 1-quart saucepan, heat apricot purée to boiling; add gelatin and sugar; stir over low heat just until dissolved; remove from heat.
2. Add lemon juice and almond extract. Set saucepan in bowl of ice cubes; stir frequently to help cool. When mixture falls in soft mounds from spoon, remove from ice.
3. Place spongecake on serving dish. With spatula, spread thin coating of apricot mixture over top and sides; refrigerate at least 10 minutes, or until coating is firm. Repeat coating and cooling twice more. During last coating, place apricot halves, cut-side up, on top of cake as pictured; glaze them with apricot mixture. Refrigerate cake at least 1 hour before serving.
4. To serve: With serrated knife, cut cake into slices. Top each slice with dessert topping, if desired. Makes 10 to 12 servings.

641.5
G

Pears Armenonville, Almond-Studded Jelly Roll, Apricot Sparkle Cake

ALMOND-STUDDED JELLY ROLL
(Pictured on page 2)

1 large package angel-food-cake mix	1 8-ounce container commercial sour cream
1 12-ounce jar apricot preserves	Canned toasted, slivered almonds
1 8-ounce package cream cheese, softened	

Make early on day:

1. Start heating oven to 350°F. Line bottoms of a 15½-by-10½-by-1-inch jelly-roll pan and an 8-inch layer-cake pan with wax paper.
2. Make up angel-food cake from mix as package label directs; put 3 cups batter in 8-inch pan. Spread remaining batter in jelly-roll pan.
3. Bake both cakes 20 minutes, or until cakes spring back when gently pressed with finger. Cool in pans 10 minutes.
4. Carefully loosen around edges with spatula; invert each on a clean towel; lift off pans. Carefully peel off paper. Store 8-inch cake for later use.
5. Roll up jelly-roll cake lightly, rolling towel up in it. Let cool thoroughly on wire rack—about 1½ hours.
6. Then unroll cake and spread surface evenly, to within about 1 inch of edges, with apricot preserves. Carefully reroll cake and place, seam side down, on serving dish.
7. In bowl blend cream cheese with sour cream; use to frost jelly roll. Into frosting stick almonds in random pattern until jelly roll is covered. Refrigerate.
8. Serve, cut into slices. Makes about 12 servings.

BANANA GINGER CAKE

1 14- or 14½-ounce package gingerbread mix	2 tablespoons confectioners' sugar
½ teaspoon unflavored gelatin	Lemon juice
2 tablespoons cold water	¾ teaspoon vanilla extract
1 cup heavy cream	5 medium-size ripe bananas
Speck salt	Coarsely-chopped walnuts

Make early on day:

1. Start heating oven to 350°F. Grease, then flour 1½-inch-deep 8-inch layer-cake pan.
2. Make up gingerbread mix as package label directs; turn into layer-cake pan.
3. Bake 30 to 35 minutes, or until cake tester, inserted in center, comes out clean. Cool in pan, on wire rack, 10 minutes; remove from pan to rack to finish cooling.
4. In small bowl sprinkle gelatin over water to soften. Scald 2 tablespoons heavy cream; pour over gelatin, stirring until gelatin is dissolved. Refrigerate until consistency of unbeaten egg white. Then, with hand beater, beat until smooth. Whip remaining cream; add salt,

sugar, ½ teaspoon lemon juice and vanilla; fold into gelatin mixture.
5. Peel bananas; dip in lemon juice. Then split cooled gingerbread, making 2 layers.
6. On cake plate place bottom layer; over it, thinly spread some of whipped cream mixture. On top of this place 4 whole bananas, parallel to each other and equidistantly apart; then move every other banana to opposite edge of cake. Cover bananas with half of remaining whipped cream; top with second layer. Spread rest of whipped cream over top. Sprinkle walnuts in center. Slice remaining banana on diagonal; place slices spoke-fashion around nuts. Refrigerate, covered.
7. At serving time, cut cake in half; then cut each half into 4 equal wedges. Makes 8 servings.

CHOCOLATE POMPADOUR

1 package active dry, or cake, yeast	1 teaspoon vanilla extract
Granulated sugar	⅔ cup unsweetened cocoa
3 cups sifted regular all-purpose flour	½ teaspoon salt
¾ cup scalded milk, cooled	1 teaspoon baking soda
¾ cup butter or margarine	½ teaspoon cinnamon
3 eggs, unbeaten	1 cup chopped blanched almonds
	Confectioners' sugar

Early on day:

1. Sprinkle or crumble yeast onto ¼ cup warm water; stir until dissolved. To yeast, in medium bowl, add 1 tablespoon granulated sugar, 2 cups flour, and milk; beat until dough is smooth and elastic. Cover with towel; let rise in warm place (80°F. to 85°F.) 40 minutes, or until doubled in bulk.
2. In large bowl, with mixer at medium speed, beat butter with 2 cups granulated sugar, eggs, and vanilla until light and fluffy; then beat in cocoa, dissolved in ½ cup warm water.
3. At low speed, add yeast mixture and remaining flour, sifted with salt, baking soda, and cinnamon. Beat about 5 minutes, then fold in almonds. Pour into well-greased 10-by-4-inch cast-aluminum bundt-cake pan.*

Let rise, covered, in warm place, about 2 hours, or until doubled in bulk.

4. Start heating oven to 350°F. When double, bake pompadour 1 hour, or until cake tester, inserted in center, comes out clean. Let stand 30 minutes, then loosen with spatula; turn out on wire rack to cool.

5. When thoroughly cool, sprinkle lightly with confectioners' sugar. Makes 16 servings.

*Available from Maid of Scandinavia, 3245 Raleigh Avenue, Minneapolis, Minnesota.

CONTINENTAL REFRIGERATOR CAKE

1 8-inch yellow-cake layer	1 to 2 tablespoons
1 cup heavy cream	granulated sugar
½ cup canned chocolate	Cut-up candied orange peel
syrup	(from a jar)
¼ cup Dutch-process cocoa	Unsweetened chocolate
2 tablespoons sweet	(about ½ square)
vermouth (optional)	

Day before:

1. Split cake layer crosswise into 2 equal layers.
2. In small bowl, with mixer or hand beater, beat cream with chocolate syrup and cocoa until consistency of frosting. Fold in vermouth and sugar.
3. Fill and top layers with chocolate-cream mixture. Sprinkle orange peel around top edge. Shave unsweetened chocolate over top. Refrigerate until served.
4. Serve, cut into wedges. Makes 6 to 8 servings.

NO-BAKE COCONUT CAKE

1 envelope unflavored	4 egg whites
gelatin	1 10-inch angel-food cake
½ cup cold water	1 cup fine-grated coconut
4 egg yolks, beaten	1 cup heavy cream
2 tablespoons regular all-	2 tablespoons granulated
purpose flour	sugar
¼ teaspoon salt	Unsweetened chocolate
2 cups milk	(about ½ square)

Day before:

1. Sprinkle gelatin over cold water to soften.
2. In saucepan combine egg yolks with flour; stir until smooth. Now stir in salt, then gradually stir in milk. Cook over low heat, stirring constantly, until custard coats back of spoon well.
3. Now stir gelatin into hot custard. Refrigerate until cool—about 1 hour.
4. Beat egg whites stiff; fold into cooled custard.
5. Tear angel-food cake into large irregular pieces; use half to cover bottom of 13-by-9-by-2-inch baking pan; pour half of custard around and over cake pieces; sprinkle with half of coconut. Repeat with remaining cake pieces and custard.
6. Whip cream with sugar; spread on top of cake;

sprinkle with rest of grated coconut; then refrigerate.

At serving time:

Grate chocolate, then sprinkle over top of cake. Serve, cut into squares. Makes 12 servings.

GRENADINE SAVARIN

1 package yellow-cake mix	2 tablespoons apricot
½ cup grenadine syrup	preserves
1 cup water	Mixed candied fruit, finely
¼ cup dark or light rum	chopped

Make early on day:

1. Start heating oven to 350°F. Generously grease and flour an 8- or 9-inch ring mold and an 8-inch layer-cake pan.
2. Make up cake mix as package label directs; fill ring mold *half full of batter;* pour rest of batter into 8-inch pan.
3. Bake both about 30 minutes, or until cake shrinks away from sides of pan; then remove from oven. (Cool layer cake and store for later use.) While still hot, invert ring mold on serving plate or cake stand with rim; unmold.
4. While cakes bake, heat syrup with water and rum. Dribble this hot syrup, very slowly, over hot ring mold, so that all areas are evenly saturated; refrigerate.
5. When Grenadine Savarin is cold, in small saucepan melt apricot preserves; press through a sieve, then spread carefully over it. Sprinkle top with candied fruit. Makes 6 to 8 servings.

DELICIOUS NO-BAKE CAKE

1 cup soft butter or	1 teaspoon vanilla extract
margarine	About 18 ladyfingers, split
2½ cups sifted	lengthwise
confectioners' sugar	½ square unsweetened
4 eggs, separated	chocolate, shaved
1 8-ounce can crushed	½ cup heavy cream,
pineapple, well drained	whipped (optional)
1 square unsweetened	
chocolate, melted	

Day before:

1. In bowl, with mixer at medium speed, blend butter with sugar until very light and fluffy, then beat in egg yolks, one at a time.
2. Beat egg whites until stiff; fold into butter mixture. Divide mixture into 3 equal parts. To one part add pineapple; to second part add melted chocolate; to third part add vanilla.
3. Line bottom of 10-by-6-by-2-inch baking dish with one third of split ladyfingers; pour on pineapple mixture. Cover with another third of ladyfingers; then spread with chocolate mixture. Top with rest of ladyfingers; spread on vanilla mixture. Refrigerate 24 hours.

About 30 minutes before serving:
Sprinkle cake with shaved chocolate. Then cut into 12 squares, wiping off knife after each cut. If desired, top each square with generous teaspoon whipped cream. Makes 12 servings.

TOFFEE-BOTTOM NUTMEG CAKE

1 1-pound package light-brown sugar	1½ teaspoons freshly-grated nutmeg
3 cups sifted regular all-purpose flour	1½ teaspoons vanilla extract
¾ cup soft butter or margarine	1½ cups commercial sour cream
½ teaspoon salt	1½ teaspoons baking soda
½ cup finely-chopped pecans	¾ cup coarsely-chopped pecans
1 egg, unbeaten	

Make day before, or early on day:
1. Start heating oven to 350°F. Grease, then lightly flour 9-inch spring-form pan.
2. In large bowl combine brown sugar with flour, butter, and salt; with pastry blender blend until smooth and crumbly. Into 3 cups of this mixture stir finely chopped pecans; press into bottom of spring-form pan.
3. Into remaining crumbly mixture stir egg, nutmeg, vanilla, and sour cream mixed with baking soda. Blend well, then pour over nut mixture in pan. Sprinkle with coarsely-chopped pecans.
4. Bake 1 hour and 35 minutes, or until cake tester, inserted in center, comes out clean. Cool in pan, on wire rack, 15 minutes.
5. Remove sides of spring-form pan; cool completely. Serve, still on bottom of pan, cut into wedges. Makes 12 servings.

FEATHERY MARBLE SPONGECAKE ✓

1 envelope unflavored gelatin	½ teaspoon salt
½ cup cold water	3 squares unsweetened chocolate, melted
4 egg yolks	½ cup boiling water
1 cup sifted confectioners' sugar	4 egg whites
1½ teaspoons vanilla extract	1 7-inch spongecake layer
	Fresh grapes (optional)

Day before, or early on day:
1. Cut 2 strips wax paper, one 16-by-8¼ inches, the other 20-by-4¼ inches. Into 9-by-5-by-3-inch loaf pan fit 16-inch strip crosswise, 20-inch strip lengthwise, so there will be a 3-inch overhang on all sides.
2. Sprinkle gelatin on cold water to soften. In medium bowl, with mixer at medium speed, beat egg yolks until thickened; gradually beat in sugar until thick and smooth, then add vanilla and salt.

3. Now beat in melted chocolate; blend well. Stir boiling water into softened gelatin; stir until gelatin is dissolved. Gradually add to chocolate mixture, beating until smooth, scraping bowl and beaters as needed.
4. In small bowl, with mixer at high speed, beat egg whites until stiff but not dry; gently fold into chocolate mixture. Pour 2 cups of this into wax-paper-lined pan.
5. Break cake layer in half; break one of halves into 1½-inch pieces, then poke them down into chocolate mixture, being sure chocolate covers cake pieces completely. Repeat with 2 more cups chocolate mixture and rest of cake, broken in pieces, being sure cake is covered. Pour any remaining chocolate mixture into pan and level off, or pour into custard cups. Refrigerate at least 5 hours.
At serving time:
Lift from pan; cut into ¾-inch slices and serve, garnished with grapes, and topped with whipped cream or dessert topping, if desired. Makes 10 servings.

JELLY-CAKE ROLL

1 large package angel-food-cake mix	1 3-ounce package raspberry-flavor gelatin
1 10-ounce package frozen raspberries, thawed	Confectioners' sugar
	Green and purple grapes (optional)
1 cup hot water	

Make cake day before:
1. Start heating oven to 350°F. Line bottom of 15½-by-10½-by-1-inch jelly-roll pan with wax paper.
2. Make up cake mix as package label directs; spread all but 3 cups batter in prepared pan.*
3. Bake 20 minutes, or until cake springs back when gently pressed with finger. Cool in pan 10 minutes, then carefully loosen around edges with spatula and invert on clean towel.
4. Now remove wax paper, then roll up cake, lightly, rolling towel up in it. Let cool thoroughly—about 1½ hours.
5. Meanwhile, drain thawed raspberries, reserving juice. In hot water, dissolve gelatin, stirring; add enough cold water to reserved raspberry juice to measure ¾ cup; stir into gelatin; add raspberries. Refrigerate until almost set, stirring occasionally.
6. When gelatin mixture is almost set, unroll cake onto wax paper; spread surface evenly to within 1 inch of edges with gelatin mixture. Tightly roll up cake; wrap wax paper tightly around it; refrigerate.
Next day, about 10 minutes before serving:
Remove cake from refrigerator; remove wax paper. Sprinkle top and sides with confectioners' sugar. Place on large serving plate with a few bunches of grapes as garnish, if desired. Serve, cut into medium-thick slices. Refrigerate extra cake slices for later use. Makes 12 servings.

*Spread 3 cups leftover angel-food-cake batter in ungreased 8-inch layer-cake pan, or spoon into 12 cupcake-pan cups with paper liners. Bake at 350°F. 15 to 20 minutes, or until done; store for later use.

COOL JEWEL DESSERT
(Pictured below)

4 cups crushed fresh straw- berries (about 4 pints)	3 envelopes unflavored gelatin
1 cup granulated sugar	¾ cup cold water
2 cups lengthwise-halved fresh strawberries (about 2 pints)	Red food color 2 7-inch spongecake layers ½ cup heavy cream

About 4 hours before serving:

1. Combine crushed strawberries with sugar; let stand 30 minutes.
2. In bottom of each of 2 8-inch layer-cake pans, arrange 1 cup halved strawberries, cut side down in pattern as pictured.
3. Sprinkle gelatin onto cold water in glass measuring cup to soften; stir over boiling water until completely dissolved. Then stir into crushed berries, along with enough food color to make mixture bright red.
4. Over and around strawberries in each pan, carefully spoon about 1¾ cups gelatin mixture, being careful to cover, but not disturb strawberry pattern (gelatin mixture should make a level layer in pan). Refrigerate 10 minutes, or until set.
5. Meanwhile, stir remaining gelatin mixture over ice until it just begins to thicken.
6. From top of each spongecake layer, with sharp knife, cut a ¼-inch thick layer; discard. Now place one of cake layers on each gelatin layer. Spoon remaining gelatin mixture around sides of each cake layer. Refrigerate until set.

Cool Jewel Dessert

About 30 minutes before serving:

1. Unmold one cake layer, pattern side up, onto serving plate. Whip cream until stiff; spread evenly over cake layer.

2. Onto chilled cookie sheet, unmold second cake layer; then carefully lift and place it, pattern side up, on top of whipped cream. Refrigerate until serving time. Serve, cut into wedges. Makes 8 to 10 servings.

Note: Four 10-ounce packages frozen sliced strawberries, thawed, *but not crushed,* may be substituted for the 4 cups crushed fresh strawberries; omit sugar in step 1. In step 4, omit stirring gelatin over ice.

MOTHER'S CHEESECAKE

16 graham crackers, crushed	1 egg, unbeaten
⅓ cup butter or margarine	1 pint commercial sour cream
3 3-ounce packages cream cheese	2 tablespoons granulated sugar
1 cup granulated sugar	1 teaspoon vanilla extract

1. Start heating oven to 350°F.

2. Mix graham-cracker crumbs with butter; press to bottom and sides of 9-inch pie plate.

3. Mix cream cheese with 1 cup sugar and egg until smooth; pour into crumb crust.

4. Bake 20 minutes; cool. Meanwhile, blend sour cream with 2 tablespoons sugar and vanilla; pour over cooled cheesecake; bake 20 minutes longer.

5. Refrigerate until well chilled; serve. This cheesecake freezes well. Makes 6 to 8 servings.

LONDONDERRY CHEESECAKE

1½ cups sifted regular all-purpose flour	1 cup finely-grated, very sharp natural Cheddar cheese
Granulated sugar	
Grated lemon peel	½ teaspoon grated orange peel
¾ cup butter or margarine	
4 egg yolks	4 eggs
Vanilla extract	¼ cup beer
4 8-ounce packages soft cream cheese	¼ cup heavy cream

Make early on day:

1. In medium bowl combine flour, 6 tablespoons sugar, and 1 teaspoon lemon peel. With pastry blender, cut in butter until crumbly; then with fork, stir in 2 egg yolks and ½ teaspoon vanilla to form a dough. Refrigerate 30 minutes.

2. Meanwhile, start heating oven to 400°F.

3. Press one third chilled dough evenly onto bottom of 9-inch spring-form pan.

4. Bake 8 to 10 minutes, or until golden brown; cool. Press rest of dough around sides of pan to within 1 inch of top.

5. In large bowl, with mixer at high speed, beat cream cheese until fluffy; gradually add cheddar cheese, beating until well blended—about 5 minutes.

6. Meanwhile, turn oven up to 500°F. Also, combine 1¾ cups sugar, ½ teaspoon vanilla, ½ teaspoon lemon peel, and orange peel; add gradually to cheese mixture, beating until smooth. Now, add eggs and 2 egg yolks, one at a time, beating well after each addition. Stir in beer and cream. Pour mixture into spring-form pan.

7. Bake 10 to 20 minutes, or until top is light brown. Then reduce oven heat to 250°F. and continue baking 2 hours, or until top is firm and cake tester, inserted in center, comes out clean.

8. Cool on wire rack, away from drafts. Remove sides of pan; wrap cake in saran; refrigerate.

At serving time:

Cut cheesecake into wedges. Makes about 12 servings.

CHEESECAKE DIVINE

1 6-ounce package zweiback	2 8-ounce packages soft cream cheese
½ cup soft butter or margarine	1 teaspoon lemon juice
¼ cup granulated sugar	2 teaspoons vanilla extract
⅛ teaspoon nutmeg	Grated peel of 1 lemon
1 envelope unflavored gelatin	1 cup heavy cream
3 eggs, separated	Fresh or frozen sliced strawberries, or canned cling peaches or pineapple chunks
½ cup granulated sugar	

Day before, or early on day:

1. Start heating oven to 400°F.

2. With rolling pin, crush zweiback into fine crumbs; mix well with butter, ¼ cup sugar, and nutmeg. Use three fourths of this mixture to firmly line bottom and sides of 9-inch spring-form pan.

3. Bake 10 minutes; cool.

4. Meanwhile, sprinkle gelatin over ½ cup cold water to soften. Blend 3 egg yolks, ½ cup sugar, and ½ cup water until smooth; cook over very low heat, *stirring constantly,* until thick—about 10 minutes. Stir in gelatin until dissolved.

5. In bowl, with mixer at medium speed, gradually beat gelatin mixture into cream cheese; then add lemon juice, vanilla, and lemon peel.

6. Lightly whip cream; blend into cheese mixture. Stiffly beat egg whites; blend into cheese mixture. Turn mixture into zwieback-lined pan; sprinkle with rest of crumbs. Refrigerate until set.

At serving time:

1. With spatula, loosen outer edges of cheesecake; remove from pan by carefully pushing up loose bottom with hands. Place, still on bottom, on serving plate.

2. Serve in wedges topped with fruit as desired. Makes 6 to 8 servings.

INDIVIDUAL CHEESECAKES
(Pictured here)

2 cups sifted regular all-purpose flour
Granulated sugar
Grated lemon peel
Vanilla extract
1 cup soft butter or margarine
3 egg yolks
2½ 8-ounce packages soft cream cheese
¼ teaspoon grated orange peel
1½ tablespoons flour
Salt
2 whole eggs
2 tablespoons heavy cream
Commercial sour cream
Strawberries, grape halves, orange
*   sections, canned pineapple chunks,*
*   maraschino cherries, walnuts, or jellies*
*   (optional)*

Day before:
1.   Mix 2 cups flour, ½ cup sugar, 2 teaspoons lemon peel, and ½ teaspoon vanilla. With pastry blender, or two knives, cut in butter and 2 egg yolks. Turn ½ cup of this mixture into each of 10 well-greased 5-ounce custard cups. Use spatula, dipped in water, to evenly spread this mixture as a lining for each cup. Refrigerate 1 hour.
2.   Meanwhile, with mixer or spoon, beat cream cheese until fluffy. Slowly add ¾ cup sugar, ⅛ teaspoon vanilla, orange peel, 1½ tablespoons flour, ⅛ teaspoon salt, and ¼ teaspoon lemon peel, beating until smooth. Add eggs and 1 egg yolk, one at a time, beating well after each addition. Beat in cream.
3.   Start heating oven to 500°F.
4.   Fill each lined custard cup with ½ cup cheese mixture.
5.   Bake 10 minutes, then turn oven down to 350°F. and continue baking 25 minutes longer. (Cracks in cheese filling are typical, so don't worry.)
6.   Cool at room temperature. Then carefully loosen with small spatula; remove and refrigerate at least 24 hours before serving.

Just before serving:
Top cheesecake with sour cream mixed with a bit of vanilla and salt. If desired, garnish sour cream with one of fruits, nuts, or jellies as pictured. Makes 10 servings.

Individual Cheesecakes

A Treat of a Torte

Hazelnut Torte

Tortes

Greek Walnut Torte

MANDARIN-ALMOND TORTE

11 tablespoons butter or margarine	½ teaspoon double-acting baking powder
1 cup granulated sugar	2 eggs, unbeaten
1 cup plus 2 tablespoons sifted regular all-purpose flour	1⅓ cups unblanched almonds, finely chopped
	1 11-ounce can Mandarin-orange sections, drained

Make day before, or early on day:
1. In small bowl, with mixer at medium speed, mix butter with ¼ cup sugar until creamy. Sift flour with baking powder; fold into butter mixture. Refrigerate this pastry, wrapped in wax paper, until cold.
2. Meanwhile, make filling: In small bowl, with mixer at high speed, beat eggs with ¾ cup sugar until light and fluffy; fold in almonds.
3. Start heating oven to 350°F. Grease and flour 9-inch layer-cake pan, or a 5-cup heart-shaped cake pan.
4. Working quickly, with fingers, press cold pastry (it is quite soft) against bottom and side of prepared pan until it stands slightly above edge of pan.
5. Heap almond mixture in pan, then fold pastry above level of filling down even with top of filling.
6. Bake 45 minutes.
7. Let cool, then unmold torte and place, almond-side up, on serving plate; decorate with orange segments. Makes 8 servings.

A TREAT OF A TORTE
(Pictured opposite)

1¼ cups sifted regular all-purpose flour	1 6-ounce package semi-sweet-chocolate pieces
¾ teaspoon baking soda	2 eggs, unbeaten
½ teaspoon salt	½ cup milk
1 8-ounce package pitted dates, snipped	½ cup orange juice
¾ cup brown sugar, firmly packed	1 cup walnuts, chopped
½ cup water	Chocolate-Cream Whip, below
½ cup butter or margarine	Green seedless grapes (optional)

Early on day:
1. Start heating oven to 350°F. Thoroughly grease, then flour 15½-by-10½-by-1-inch jelly-roll pan.
2. Onto wax paper sift flour with baking soda and salt.
3. In large saucepan combine dates, brown sugar, water, and butter; cook, over low heat, stirring constantly, until dates soften. Remove from heat and immediately stir in chocolate pieces; stir until melted.
4. Now, with spoon, beat in eggs. Then alternately beat in flour mixture and milk and orange juice. Stir in nuts. Pour into prepared pan.
5. Bake 25 to 30 minutes, or until top springs back when gently pressed with finger. Let cool in pan 15 minutes, then loosen with spatula and turn out on wire racks to finish cooling.
6. Meanwhile, make Chocolate-Cream Whip.
7. When torte is thoroughly cool, cut it crosswise into three pieces, each 5 inches wide. On oblong tray place 1 of pieces; spread with one third Chocolate-Cream Whip. Repeat with other two pieces, frosting top as pictured. Refrigerate until ready to serve.
8. At serving time, garnish tray with grapes, if desired. Serve torte, cut into 1-inch-thick slices; then cut in half crosswise, if desired. Makes 10 or 20 servings.

CHOCOLATE-CREAM WHIP: In small saucepan combine ½ cup semisweet-chocolate pieces with 2 tablespoons liquid honey, and 1 tablespoon water. Stir over low heat until chocolate is melted; remove from heat. Stir in ½ teaspoon vanilla extract, then cool until slightly thickened. In bowl combine 1 cup heavy cream and ⅛ teaspoon salt, then beat until thick and soft peaks form; gently fold in chocolate mixture.

HAZELNUT TORTE
(Pictured opposite)

1¼ pounds shelled hazelnuts (4 cups)	1 cup shortening
10 egg whites	3½ cups sifted confectioners' sugar
2 cups granulated sugar	4 egg yolks
⅔ cup sifted cake flour	3 tablespoons instant coffee powder
1 cup soft butter or margarine	1½ teaspoons hot water

Make early on day before serving:
1. Finely grind 2 cups hazelnuts.
2. Start heating oven to 275°F.
3. On each of 3 squares wax paper draw a 9-inch circle. Grease wax paper to a point slightly beyond circle line, then flour lightly. Place one of prepared wax-paper squares on each of 2 lightly greased cookie sheets; reserve third square for later use.
4. Beat egg whites until stiff but not dry; then gradually beat in 1½ cups granulated sugar, beating until stiff. Gently fold in ground hazelnuts and flour, blending carefully.
5. Spread one third of hazelnut mixture just to edge of circle line on each of 2 wax-paper squares, keeping sides of circles even. Refrigerate rest of hazelnut mixture.
6. Bake 2 circles 1 hour, or until light brown and dry, switching cookie sheets after 30 minutes. When done, invert each on wire rack; peel off paper; turn right side up and let cool.
7. Now place third wax-paper square on cooled cookie sheet; spread with rest of hazelnut mixture as in step 5; bake and cool as in step 6.
8. Now turn oven heat up to 400°F. Bake 2 cups whole hazelnuts in shallow baking pan 10 minutes,

shaking pan occasionally. Then rub off skin from 24 of them.

9.   Butter large piece wax paper. In small skillet, over medium heat, melt ½ cup granulated sugar to a golden syrup, stirring occasionally with a fork. Into syrup drop the 24 hazelnuts, a few at a time, coating all sides. Then drain, lifting one by one with fork to buttered wax paper.

10.   Finely grind rest of baked hazelnuts. In large bowl, with mixer at medium speed, cream butter with shortening until well blended; gradually beat in confectioners' sugar, blending well. Now add egg yolks, one at a time, beating until light and fluffy; beat in 1¼ cups ground hazelnuts.

11.   Refrigerate ½ cup of this frosting. Into another 1¼ cups frosting stir instant coffee dissolved in hot water; refrigerate.

12.   Now stack the three baked layers, filling and frosting them with the rest of frosting. Refrigerate 1 hour, then sprinkle top and pat sides with rest of ground hazelnuts.

13.   With coffee frosting in decorating bag with number 3 tube in place, press out continuous border of half circles around top edge of torte; repeat, about 1 inch in from this border. Make one large rosette in center.

14.   Next, with ½ cup refrigerated frosting in decorating bag with same tube in place, press out small rosette wherever half circles join each other and where they join center rosette. Top each of these rosettes with glazed hazelnut as pictured.

15.   With 2 large spatulas, transfer torte to cake plate; refrigerate until served. Makes about 16 wedge-shaped servings.

APRICOT-GLAZED WINE TORTE

3 9-inch spongecake layers	8 pecan halves
2 10-ounce jars apricot preserves	6 pecan quarters
1 cup muscat wine	Canned apricot halves
⅔ cup finely-chopped pecans	Feathery fern (optional)

Make day before:

1.   With serrated knife, split each spongecake layer in half horizontally, making 6 layers in all. On 14-inch cake plate, lay one layer, crust side down; spread with ⅓ cup preserves; top with second layer; sprinkle evenly with ⅓ cup wine, then with ⅓ cup finely chopped pecans. Repeat with next three layers.

2.   Top with last layer, crust side up; sprinkle with ⅓ cup wine. In heavy saucepan, over medium-high heat, melt 1 cup preserves. With pastry brush, use melted preserves to glaze side of torte. Decorate top with remaining preserves, pecan halves and quarters. Refrigerate until next day.

Just before serving:

Arrange apricot halves, rounded side up, on cake plate around torte, with fern tucked in at intervals, if desired. Makes 12 servings.

TOFFEE TORTE

Sifted regular all-purpose flour	1 cup heavy cream
Salt	1 cup milk
Butter or margarine	2 egg yolks, unbeaten
¾ cup dark-brown sugar, firmly packed	Brandy
	1 teaspoon vanilla extract
	Granulated sugar

Make pastry and filling day before:

1.   Sift 1½ cups flour with ¼ teaspoon salt. With pastry blender, or 2 knives, scissor fashion, cut in ¾ cup butter until like coarse corn meal. Add 3 tablespoons water and toss quickly together, forming a smooth ball. Wrap this pastry in wax paper; refrigerate.

2.   In small saucepan combine brown sugar, 2 tablespoons flour, and ½ teaspoon salt. Gradually stir in ½ cup cream and milk. Bring to boil, stirring, then boil 1 minute. Remove from heat.

3.   Start heating oven to 300°F.

4.   In small bowl beat egg yolks; gradually add sugar-milk mixture, beating constantly. Return to saucepan; bring to boil, stirring, then boil 1 minute. Remove from heat; stir in 1 tablespoon butter, 2 tablespoons brandy, and vanilla. Lay wax paper directly on surface of this filling; refrigerate.

5.   Lightly flour large cookie sheet. On it roll a little more than half of pastry into 10-inch circle. Trim edges with knife or pastry wheel. Prick with fork, then sprinkle with 1 tablespoon granulated sugar.

6.   Bake about 30 minutes, or until golden. Let cool slightly, then remove to wire rack to finish cooling. Cover with wax paper until ready to use.

7.   While first pastry circle is baking, lightly flour second cookie sheet. On it roll out rest of pastry into 9½-inch circle; trim edges. Cut circle into 12 equal wedges; prick with fork; sprinkle with 1 tablespoon granulated sugar, then refrigerate. When 10-inch circle is done, bake these pastry wedges as in step 6.

About 1 hour before serving:
1. Lay 10-inch pastry circle on serving plate; spread with filling to within ½ inch from edge. On filling place, equidistantly, 10 of pastry wedges (reserve other 2 wedges for nibbling).
2. Beat ½ cup cream with 1 tablespoon brandy until stiff; put in decorating bag with number 5 tube in place; use to pipe decorative edge on sides of pastry; or drop whipped cream by teaspoonfuls on edge. Refrigerate at least 30 minutes before serving. Serve, cut into wedges. Makes 10 servings.

GREEK WALNUT TORTE
(Pictured on page 10)

9 eggs, separated	½ teaspoon ground cloves
1 cup granulated sugar	½ teaspoon salt
3 cups ground walnuts	2 teaspoons double-acting
½ cup packaged dried	baking powder
bread crumbs	1 teaspoon vanilla extract
1 tablespoon grated orange	½ cup water
peel	Brandy Butter Cream, below
2 teaspoons grated lemon	⅔ cup coarsely-broken
peel	walnuts
1 teaspoon cinnamon	

Make day before, or early on day:
1. Start heating oven to 350°F. Line bottoms of 3 8-inch layer-cake pans with wax paper.
2. In medium bowl, with mixer at high speed, beat egg yolks with sugar until very thick and light colored.
3. In very large bowl stir together ground walnuts, crumbs, orange and lemon peels, cinnamon, cloves, salt, and baking powder. Mix vanilla with water and egg yolks; stir into walnut mixture.
4. In large bowl, with mixer at high speed, beat egg whites until stiff but not dry. Fold gently into walnut batter until thoroughly combined. Pour into prepared pans.
5. Bake 30 minutes, or until cake tester, inserted in center, comes out clean. Invert layers, in pans, on wire racks to cool.
6. Loosen each layer around edges and turn out of pan; remove wax paper. Wrap cooled layers and store at room temperature.
Several hours before serving:
Make up Brandy Butter Cream. Use to fill and frost layers; then lightly press broken walnuts into frosting on top of torte as pictured. Refrigerate until serving. Serve with grapes and oranges, if desired. Makes 8 to 12 servings.

BRANDY BUTTER CREAM: In small bowl, with mixer at medium speed, beat ½ cup butter or margarine until creamy. Beat in ⅛ teaspoon salt and 1 1-pound package confectioners' sugar; then beat in 1 egg, 1 teaspoon vanilla extract, and 2 tablespoons brandy.

Pies

FLAKY PASTRY FOR 2-CRUST PIE

2¼ cups sifted regular	3 teaspoons finely-grated
all-purpose flour	lemon peel (optional)
1 teaspoon salt	5 tablespoons cold water
¾ cup plus 2 tablespoons	
vegetable shortening	

1. In bowl combine flour and salt. With pastry blender or 2 knives, cut in shortening until mixture is size of peas. Stir in lemon peel, if desired.
2. Blend ⅓ cup of this mixture with water. Add to rest of flour mixture, then, with fork or fingers, mix until dough holds together.
3. Shape dough into flat round, then divide in half; form into 2 balls. (If very warm day, wrap and refrigerate up to 30 minutes.) Place 1 ball of pastry on lightly floured surface. With stockinet-covered rolling pan, flatten gently. Then roll lightly, from center out to edge in all directions, forming circle about 1½ inch larger than inverted 8- or 9-inch pie plate. (Be sure to lift rolling pin near edge of circle, to keep from splitting or getting thin. If edge splits, pinch cracks together. If pastry sticks, loosen gently with spatula.)
4. Fold pastry circle in half; lift onto ungreased pie plate with seam at center; unfold. Use bent index finger to fit pastry gently into pie plate.
5. Repeat step 3 with other ball of pastry. Arrange desired filling in lined pie plate. Trim bottom crust even with edge of pie plate. Now fold top crust in half; with knife make several slits near center of seam, so steam can escape.
6. Moisten edge of lower crust with water. Lay top crust on top of filling with seam at center; unfold. With kitchen scissors, trim top crust ½ inch beyond edge of pie plate; fold edge of top crust under edge of bottom crust; press together. Finish edge as desired. Bake as directed in recipe.

FOR 8- OR 9-INCH PIE SHELL: Use 1½ cups flour, ½ teaspoon salt, ½ cup shortening, 1½ teaspoons lemon peel, and ¼ cup water. Prepare pastry as directed; roll out and fit into pie plate as for bottom crust, trimming to within 1 inch of edge of pie plate. Turn edge under; then turn pastry up to make a stand-up rim. Finish edge as desired. Then, with 4-tined fork, prick pastry, close and deep, over bottom and sides. Refrigerate 30 minutes. If recipe calls for baked pie shell, bake at 450°F. 12 to 15 minutes, or until golden, pricking well after 5 minutes to prevent puffing. Cool.

EASY BAKED PIE SHELL

For 8- or 9-inch pie shell:
1⅓ cups sifted regular all-purpose flour
½ teaspoon salt
⅓ cup salad oil
2 tablespoons cold water

For 6-inch pie shell:
⅔ cup sifted regular all-purpose flour
¼ teaspoon salt
2 tablespoons plus 2 teaspoons salad oil
1 tablespoon cold water

About 1 hour and 30 minutes before needed:
1. Start heating oven to 450°F.
2. Combine flour with salt. With fork, thoroughly stir in salad oil. Sprinkle cold water over mixture; mix well. Mold dough firmly into ball. (If too dry, mix in 1 to 2 teaspoons more salad oil.)
3. Immediately roll dough between two pieces wax paper to about ⅛-inch thickness. (To prevent paper from slipping, wipe kitchen counter or board with damp cloth.) Peel off top paper; place pastry in pie plate; with wax paper on top. Peel off paper; fit pastry loosely into pie plate. Trim pastry to within 1 inch of edge of pie plate; fold this overhang under; flute edge as desired. With 4-tined fork, thoroughly prick bottom and sides of pastry.
4. Bake 12 to 15 minutes, or until light golden-brown. Cool. Fill as desired.

APPLE PIE WITH A DIFFERENCE

4 medium apples
Granulated sugar
Cinnamon
⅛ teaspoon nutmeg
⅛ teaspoon ground cloves
⅛ teaspoon salt
1 tablespoon lemon juice
2 teaspoons grated lemon peel
3 tablespoons butter or margarine
3 tablespoons regular all-purpose flour
1 cup apple cider
½ cup light raisins
1 package piecrust mix
1 egg white
3 tablespoons chopped walnuts

Early on day, or about 2 hours before serving:
1. Coarsely grate pared apples into bowl, making about 3 cups shreds; stir in ½ cup sugar, ½ teaspoon cinnamon, nutmeg, cloves, salt, lemon juice and peel.
2. In large saucepan, melt butter; then blend in flour to form smooth paste. Add apple cider, a little at a time, stirring constantly; cook, over medium heat, until mixture is thickened and glossy. Add apple mixture and raisins; bring to boil; cool.
3. Meanwhile, make up piecrust mix as package label directs. Roll out bottom crust and fit to 9-inch pie plate, making fluted or rope edge. With pastry brush, brush pie shell with some of egg white beaten with 1 teaspoon water. Roll out rest of pastry; then, with pastry wheel, cut out 3 strips, two of them 7 inches long, and one about 8½ inches long.

4. Start heating oven to 350°F.
5. Spoon apple filling into pie shell. Lay the 3 pastry strips across top of pie, leaving spaces in between; brush pastry strips with rest of egg-white-water mixture.
6. In small bowl combine walnuts, 1 tablespoon sugar, and ¼ teaspoon cinnamon. Sprinkle this mixture on top of pie between pastry strips.
7. Bake about 40 minutes, or until crust is golden-brown and filling is bubbly.
8. Let pie cool on wire rack. Serve warm, cut into 8 wedges.

FRESH BERRY PIE

Flaky Pastry for 2-Crust Pie, page 13
⅔ to ¾ cup granulated sugar
2 tablespoons regular all-purpose flour, or 1½ tablespoons quick-cooking tapioca
½ teaspoon grated lemon peel
1 to 2 teaspoons lemon juice
¼ teaspoon nutmeg
½ teaspoon cinnamon
⅛ teaspoon salt
2 cups fresh blueberries, blackberries, raspberries, loganberries, or boysenberries
1 tablespoon butter or margarine

1. Start heating oven 425°F.
2. Line a 9-inch pie plate with bottom pastry crust; roll out top crust.
3. Combine sugar, flour, lemon peel, lemon juice, nutmeg, cinnamon, and salt.
4. Arrange half of berries in pie plate; sprinkle with half of sugar mixture; repeat. Dot filling with butter; adjust top crust; seal edges.
5. Bake 40 to 50 minutes, or until filling is tender and crust nicely browned. Serve warm or cold. Makes 8 servings.

PEACH OR PLUM PIE: Substitute sliced, peeled peaches or sliced plums for berries. Proceed as above.

CREAMY CARAMEL PIE ✓

Favorite pastry (or packaged piecrust mix) for 9-inch pie shell
Unflavored gelatin
Water
2 8-ounce packages cream cheese
6 tablespoons granulated sugar
3 egg yolks, unbeaten
¼ cup lemon juice
1 teaspoon vanilla extract
½ cup vanilla-caramel sauce (about half a 10-ounce jar)
¼ cup walnut halves, broken

Day before, or early on day:
1. Prepare pastry; use to line 9-inch pie plate; make high, fluted edge. Refrigerate 20 minutes.
2. Start heating oven to 450°F.
3. Bake pie shell about 10 minutes, or until golden,

pricking well after 5 minutes to prevent puffing; cool on wire rack.

4. Sprinkle 1½ teaspoons gelatin over ¼ cup water to soften; then stir, over hot water, to dissolve. Now, in medium bowl, with mixer at medium speed, beat cream cheese until fluffy; gradually beat in sugar until dissolved; add egg yolks, lemon juice, vanilla, and gelatin. Pour filling into cooled pie shell; refrigerate until set.

5. In small saucepan, sprinkle ½ teaspoon gelatin over 2 tablespoons water to soften; stir over low heat until gelatin is dissolved; blend in caramel sauce. Refrigerate a few minutes to cool.

6. Spoon sauce over top of pie, then sprinkle walnuts around top edge. Refrigerate until caramel topping is set. Makes 8 servings.

HALF 'N' HALF CHEESE PIE

Favorite pastry (or packaged piecrust mix) for 9-inch pie shell	½ cup water
	1 8-ounce package cream cheese
2 squares unsweetened chocolate	¼ cup milk
	¾ cup granulated sugar
2 teaspoons unflavored gelatin	1 teaspoon rum extract
	1 cup heavy cream (½ pint)

Day before, or early on day:

1. Prepare pastry; use to line 9-inch pie plate; make rope edge. Refrigerate about 20 minutes.
2. Start heating oven to 450°F.
3. Bake pie shell about 10 minutes, or until golden, pricking well after 5 minutes to prevent puffing. Cool on wire rack.
4. Melt 1 square chocolate; set aside. In measuring cup sprinkle gelatin over water to soften; then set cup in hot water; stir until gelatin is dissolved.
5. In medium bowl, with mixer at medium speed, beat cream cheese until smooth; blend in milk, sugar, and gelatin. Pour 1½ cups of this mixture into bowl; beat in melted chocolate; pour into cooled pie shell; refrigerate until set.
6. Stir rum extract into remaining cheese mixture. Whip cream, then gently fold into cheese mixture.

Spoon on top of set chocolate layer; refrigerate until set.
7. Garnish with chocolate curls, made from remaining square of chocolate. Serve, cut into 8 wedges.

CRANBERRY MERINGUE PIE

1 baked 9-inch pie shell	¼ teaspoon nutmeg
Granulated sugar	Salt
3 tablespoons cornstarch	¼ cup butter or margarine
½ teaspoon grated lemon peel	½ cup water
	4 cups fresh cranberries
1½ teaspoons lemon juice	3 egg whites, unbeaten

Several hours before serving:

1. Make and bake pie shell.
2. In large saucepan combine ¾ cup sugar, cornstarch, lemon peel and juice, nutmeg, ⅛ teaspoon salt, butter, water, and cranberries. Simmer slowly, uncovered, until all cranberry skins pop. Cool slightly, pour into baked pie shell; refrigerate until set.

About 1 hour before serving:

1. Start heating oven to 350°F.
2. In medium bowl, with mixer at high speed, beat egg whites with ¼ teaspoon salt until frothy. Gradually add 6 tablespoons sugar, beating until stiff peaks are formed. With spoon, place mounds of this meringue around top edge of cranberry filling, make sure it touches inner edge of crust all around. Heap rest of meringue in center, making attractive points.
3. Bake 12 to 15 minutes, or until nicely browned. Cool away from drafts.

To flame: Just before serving pie, sprinkle it with 3 tablespoons warm brandy; ignite with match, then carry, flaming, to the table.

LEMON MERINGUE PIE

1 baked 8-inch pie shell	3 egg yolks, slightly beaten
Granulated sugar	
¼ cup cornstarch	1 tablespoon butter or margarine
Salt	
1¼ cups warm water	3 egg whites, at room temperature
Grated peel of 1 lemon	
¼ cup lemon juice	

1. Make, bake, and cool pie shell.
2. In double-boiler top, combine 1 cup sugar, cornstarch, and ⅛ teaspoon salt. Slowly stir in water, then lemon peel and juice. Now add egg yolks and butter. Cook, over boiling water, stirring constantly, until smooth and thick enough to mound when dropped from spoon. Remove from heat; lay piece of wax paper directly on surface of filling; refrigerate.
3. In medium bowl, with mixer at high speed, beat egg whites with ¼ teaspoon salt until frothy. Now sprinkle 6 tablespoons sugar, 1 tablespoon at a time, over egg whites, beating thoroughly after each addition. (This

method of adding sugar and beating dissolves sugar and help prevent "beading.")

4. Continue sprinkling and beating egg whites until all sugar is added; then continue beating until stiff peaks form. (To test meringue for stiff peaks, slowly withdraw beaters and hold up; meringue should form pointed peaks that stand upright and don't curl over.)

5. Start heating oven to 425°F.

6. Remove wax paper from cooled filling; spread filling evenly in cooled pie shell.

7. Now, with spoon, place mounds of meringue around outside edge of filling; with spatula, spread meringue so it touches inner edge of pie shell all around, to prevent shrinking. Then heap rest of meringue in center of filling and spread out to meet meringue border. With spatula, pull up points on meringue to make attractive top.

8. Bake 3 to 4 minutes, or until golden. Cool pie on wire rack, away from drafts.

9. To cut meringue neatly, first dip knife into hot water; then shake off excess drops and cut pie into 6 wedges.

SCINTILLATING LEMON PIE
(Pictured opposite)

Favorite pastry (or packaged piecrust mix) for 2-crust pie	¼ teaspoon salt
1½ tablespoons medium-crystal sugar*	⅓ cup soft butter or margarine
1 teaspoon nutmeg	3 eggs, well beaten
1½ cups granulated sugar	2 tablespoons grated lemon peel
3 tablespoons regular all-purpose flour	3 peeled lemons, very thinly sliced
	½ cup cold water

Early on day:

1. Start heating oven to 400°F.

2. Prepare pastry; roll out half of pastry; use to line 9-inch pie plate, making high, stand-up, fluted edge; refrigerate until needed.

3. On lightly floured surface, roll out other half of pastry to a 9-inch circle. On it invert 8-inch pie plate or bowl; with pastry wheel or sharp knife, trace around pie plate, cutting through pastry. Cut circle into 6 equal wedges.

4. With wide spatula, lift pastry wedges to cookie sheet; sprinkle with combined medium-crystal sugar and nutmeg. Bake 10 minutes, or until lightly browned; set aside to cool.

5. Bake 10 minutes, or until lightly browned; set aside to cool.

6. Meanwhile, in bowl, stir granulated sugar with flour, salt, butter, eggs, lemon peel, sliced lemons, and cold water; carefully pour into pie shell.

7. Bake 25 minutes. Then on pie, place 3 pastry wedges, equally separated, with points touching at cen-

ter as pictured. Bake 10 minutes longer; cool. (The 3 extra pastry wedges are for nibbling.)

8. Serve pie, cut into 6 wedges.

*Available at bakery supply house. Granulated sugar may be substituted.

LEMON-CHEESE CUSTARD PIE

Favorite pastry (or packaged piecrust mix) for 2-crust pie	½ cup lemon juice
3 eggs, unbeaten	1 8-ounce package cream cheese
⅔ cup granulated sugar	2 teaspoons grated lemon peel

Day before:

1. Prepare pastry; use to line 9-inch pie plate, then trim overhang even with edge of plate. From remaining pastry, rolled out, cut about 78 1-inch hearts. Moisten pastry rim with water, then press hearts onto rim, overlapping slightly. Refrigerate about 20 minutes.

2. Start heating oven to 450°F.

3. Bake pie shell about 10 minutes, or until golden, pricking well after 5 minutes to prevent puffing; cool.

4. With mixer at medium speed, beat eggs in double-boiler top until fluffy. Place double-boiler top over hot water, then continue beating, gradually adding sugar, then lemon juice. Cook, stirring constantly, until custard is thick and smooth and mounds when dropped from spoon. Remove from hot water.

5. In medium bowl, with mixer at medium speed, beat cream cheese until light and fluffy. With rubber spatula or spoon, gradually blend in custard and lemon peel. Pour into cooled pie shell; then, with spatula, spread custard up to lower edge of hearts; refrigerate.

At serving time:

Sprinkle pie around edge with more grated lemon peel, if desired. Serve, cut into 8 wedges.

LEMON-WALNUT PIE

½ package piecrust mix	1 cup milk
1 cup granulated sugar	1 teaspoon grated lemon peel
2 tablespoons regular all-purpose flour	3 egg whites, stiffly beaten
¼ cup melted butter or margarine	½ cup walnut halves
3 egg yolks, well beaten	Sugared lemon slices
¼ cup lemon juice	

Early on day:

1. Start heating oven to 450°F.

2. Prepare piecrust mix as package label directs for 9-inch pie shell.

3. Bake pie shell 8 minutes, then remove from oven. Reduce oven temperature to 350°F.

4. In medium bowl combine sugar, flour, butter, egg yolks, and lemon juice; with mixer at medium speed,

Scintillating Lemon Pie

beat until light and fluffy, then add milk and beat, at low speed, just until blended. Fold in lemon peel and egg whites. Pour mixture into pie shell; arrange walnut halves in "spoke-wheel" pattern on top.

5. Bake about 35 minutes, or until filling is set. Cool on wire rack; refrigerate.

6. At serving time, with sharp knife, cut pie into 6 to 8 wedges; garnish each wedge with sugared lemon slice, if desired.

KAHLUA PIE

1 package piecrust mix	4 egg whites
Egg white	¼ teaspoon salt
4½ teaspoons unflavored gelatin	¼ cup granulated sugar
⅓ cup granulated sugar	1¼ cups heavy cream
4 egg yolks	Unsweetened chocolate
¾ cup Kahlua (coffee-flavor liqueur)	(about ½ square)

Early on day:

1. Make up piecrust mix as package label directs for 2-crust pie. Roll out half of piecrust and fit into 8-inch glass pie plate, using kitchen scissors to trim edge even with edge of pie plate; secure to rim of pie plate with a little egg white. Roll out other half of piecrust; then, with sharp knife, cut into strips about ½ inch wide.

2. Brush top edge of pie shell with egg white, then fasten one end of pastry strip to edge. Holding end of pencil at right angle to pie plate edge, make loop by lifting strip over pencil; remove pencil; then press strip with side of pencil to seal loop in upright position. Repeat all around edge of pie, using additional strips as needed. Refrigerate.

3. Start heating oven to 450°F.

4. Using 4-tined fork, prick pie shell well, then bake 12 to 15 minutes, or until golden; prick again after 5 minutes if bubbles appear; cool.

5. Meanwhile, in double-boiler top, combine gelatin and ⅓ cup sugar; add egg yolks and beat slightly; now stir in Kahlua. Cook, over boiling water, stirring constantly, until thickened; cool.

6. Now, in large bowl, beat egg whites until frothy; add salt and beat until soft peaks form; gradually beat in ¼ cup sugar.

7. Whip 1 cup cream until stiff; place on top of egg whites, then top with cooled Kahlua mixture; gently fold mixtures together. Refrigerate until mixture mounds when dropped from spoon; then pile gently in cooled pie shell. Refrigerate.

About 30 minutes before serving:

Whip ¼ cup heavy cream and drop, by rounded table-spoonfuls, onto top of pie. Sprinkle with shaved unsweetened chocolate. Refrigerate; serve, cut into 8 wedges.

PINK-OF-PERFECTION PIE

Favorite pastry (or packaged piecrust mix) for 8-inch pie shell	¼ cup white crème de cacao
4½ teaspoons unflavored gelatin	Red food color
⅓ cup granulated sugar	4 egg whites
4 egg yolks	¼ teaspoon salt
½ cup crème de noyaux liqueur	¼ cup granulated sugar
	1¼ cups heavy cream

Early on day:

1. Make and bake pie shell with high fluted edge; cool.

2. In double-boiler top combine gelatin and ⅓ cup sugar; add egg yolks and beat slightly. Now stir in crème de noyaux and crème de cacao; cook, over boiling water, stirring constantly, until mixture thickens—about 5 minutes. Remove from heat and stir until cool—about 10 minutes. Then stir in few drops food color to tint deep pink.

3. In large bowl beat egg whites until frothy; add salt and beat until soft peaks form. Gradually beat in ¼ cup sugar.

4. Now whip 1 cup cream until stiff; pour onto beaten egg whites; then gently pour on gelatin mixture; with rubber spatula, gently fold mixtures together. Refrigerate 30 minutes, or until mixture mounds when dropped from spoon.

5. Now, using rubber spatula, lightly pile mixture in cooled pie shell; refrigerate again.

About 30 minutes before serving:

Whip ¼ cup cream; put in decorating bag with number 30 tube in place. Pipe 4 lines across top of pie, dividing it into 8 wedges. Where lines cross in center, press out a large rosette. Refrigerate until ready to serve. Makes 8 servings.

MAPLE-NUT WHIP PIE

1 baked 8-inch pie shell	1 cup heavy cream
1 envelope unflavored gelatin	3 egg whites
¼ cup cold water	½ teaspoon salt
3 egg yolks	1 tablespoon confectioners' sugar
¾ cup maple or maple-flavored syrup	1 cup broken walnuts or other nuts

Early on day, or 4 hours before serving:

1. Make and bake pie shell with high, fluted edge; cool.

2. Sprinkle gelatin over cold water; stir until gelatin is dissolved.

3. In double boiler, beat egg yolks with maple syrup until well blended. Cook, over boiling water, stirring constantly, until slightly thickened—about 5 minutes. Add gelatin mixture; stir until dissolved. Remove from

heat; pour into large bowl; refrigerate until consistency of unbeaten egg whites, stirring occasionally.

4. Now whip cream until stiff. Beat egg whites with salt until stiff but not dry; fold in confectioners' sugar.

5. Into gelatin mixture fold whipped cream, then egg whites, and ¾ cup nuts. Pour into cooled pie shell; refrigerate until set—about 2 hours. Then sprinkle ¼ cup nuts around edge.

6. Serve, cut into 6 wedges.

CRUMBLY PECAN-PEACH PIE

1 package piecrust mix
2 1-pound 13-ounce cans cling-peach slices
¼ cup light-brown sugar
2 tablespoons soft butter or margarine
⅓ cup chopped pecans
⅛ teaspoon cinnamon

A few hours before serving:

1. Prepare piecrust mix as package label directs for 9-inch pie shell with fluted or rope edge. Reserve rest of piecrust mix.

2. Start heating oven to 375°F.

3. Drain peach slices well on paper towels, then arrange them, side by side, over bottom and up sides of pie shell.

4. In small bowl, with fork, mix remaining piecrust mix with brown sugar, butter, pecans and cinnamon; sprinkle evenly over peaches.

5. Bake 1 hour, or until topping is light brown. Cool on wire rack, then serve. Makes 8 servings.

PUMPKIN CHIFFON PIE

1 baked 9-inch pie shell
1 envelope unflavored gelatin
¾ cup brown sugar, packed
½ teaspoon salt
½ teaspoon nutmeg
½ teaspoon cinnamon
¼ teaspoon ginger
2 egg yolks
1 cup undiluted evaporated milk
½ cup cold water
1¼ cups canned pumpkin
2 egg whites

Early on day:

1. Make and bake pie shell; cool.

2. Combine gelatin, ½ cup brown sugar, salt, nutmeg, cinnamon, and ginger.

3. In double-boiler top beat egg yolks; stir in evaporated milk, water, pumpkin, then gelatin mixture; cook, over boiling water, stirring constantly, 10 minutes. Refrigerate, stirring occasionally, until like unbeaten egg white.

4. Beat egg whites until fairly stiff; gradually add ¼ cup brown sugar, beating until stiff; fold in pumpkin mixture. Turn into cooled pie shell; refrigerate until set (6 to 8 hours).

5. Serve pie topped with whipped cream and chopped walnuts, if desired; garnish with tiny bunches of grapes. Cut into 6 to 8 wedges.

RASPBERRY DREAM PIE

½ package piecrust mix
1 10-ounce package frozen raspberries, thawed
1 regular package raspberry-flavor gelatin
1 cup boiling water
2 tablespoons granulated sugar
1 cup heavy cream, whipped, or whipped dessert topping

Make day before, or early on day:

1. Start heating oven to 400°F.

2. Prepare pastry from mix as package label directs; roll into 8-inch circle; use to line 6-inch pie plate. Make rope edge ¾ inches high; with fork, prick pie shell well.

3. Bake 20 minutes, or until golden; cool.

4. Drain raspberries, reserving juice. Stir gelatin into boiling water until dissolved. To reserved raspberry juice add enough water to measure ¾ cup; stir into gelatin with sugar and raspberries. Refrigerate until mixture mounds when dropped from spoon.

5. Fold in whipped cream; refrigerate again until mixture is firm enough to mound. Spoon about 1½ cups of filling into cooled pie shell; spoon rest into small mold or custard cups; refrigerate. Makes 1 6-inch pie (2 or 3 servings) and dessert for another day.

FOR 8-INCH PIE: Make, bake, and cool 8-inch pie shell as package label directs; then use all of raspberry-gelatin mixture as filling.

RASPBERRY-BURGUNDY PIE

1 baked 8-inch pie shell
1 teaspoon unflavored gelatin
Cold water
1 4¾-ounce package currant-raspberry Danish dessert
2 tablespoons lemon juice
½ cup Burgundy wine
1 10-ounce package frozen raspberries, partially thawed
Vanilla ice cream, dessert topping, or whipped cream (optional)

Early on day:

1. Make and bake pie shell; cool.

2. Sprinkle gelatin on 2 tablespoons cold water to soften.

3. Into Danish dessert, in medium saucepan, stir 6 tablespoons cold water, lemon juice, and Burgundy. Bring mixture to boil; boil 1 minute, stirring constantly. Remove from heat and add gelatin, stirring until blended. Then stir in raspberries. Pour at once into cooled pie shell; refrigerate at least 4 hours.

Just before serving:
Garnish pie with small scoops ice cream, dessert topping, or whipped cream, if desired. Serve, cut into 6 to 8 wedges.

RHUBARB CREAM-CHEESE PIE

1 package piecrust mix	1 8-ounce package cream
⅓ cup granulated sugar	cheese, softened
3 tablespoons cornstarch	2 eggs, unbeaten
2 12-ounce packages frozen	½ cup granulated sugar
rhubarb, partially	1 cup commercial sour
thawed	cream
	Unblanched almonds

Make early on day:
1. Start heating oven to 425°F.
2. Prepare pastry from piecrust mix as package label directs for 9-inch pie shell, making fluted or rope edge. Set aside.
3. In medium saucepan mix ⅓ cup sugar, cornstarch, and rhubarb; cook, over medium heat, stirring, until thickened. Pour into pie shell.
4. Bake 10 minutes.
5. Meanwhile, in small bowl, with mixer at medium speed, beat cream cheese, eggs, and ½ cup sugar until smooth; pour over rhubarb. Turn oven down to 350°F. Bake pie 30 minutes; cool.
6. When pie is cool, spread top with sour cream; then garnish top with 2 circular rows of almonds. Makes 8 servings.

PEACHY-STRAWBERRY PIE

1 baked 9-inch pie shell	2 tablespoons cornstarch
1 8-ounce package cream	1 quart fresh strawberries
cheese, softened	2 tablespoons lemon juice
Granulated sugar	Red food color
¼ teaspoon salt	1 16-ounce can cling-peach
1 tablespoon milk	slices, drained
½ teaspoon vanilla extract	

Early on day:
1. Make and bake pie shell; cool.
2. In medium bowl, with mixer at medium speed, thoroughly blend cream cheese, 3 tablespoons sugar, salt, milk, and vanilla. Spread this mixture over bottom and up sides of cooled pie shell, bringing it well up on sides; refrigerate.
3. In saucepan blend ½ cup sugar with cornstarch; add 1½ cups strawberries, crushed, and lemon juice.

Cook, stirring constantly, until clear and thickened. Stir in enough food color to make bright red; then stir in 1½ cups strawberries, sliced; let cool.
4. Into cheese-lined pie shell spoon about three-fourths of cooled strawberry mixture; on top arrange peach slices; then cover peaches with remaining strawberry mixture. Refrigerate at least 4 hours.
5. Serve, cut into 8 wedges.

DEVONSHIRE STRAWBERRY PIE

1 baked 9-inch pie shell	2 tablespoons granulated
1 envelope unflavored	sugar
gelatin	⅛ teaspoon salt
¼ cup water	2 egg whites
1 cup commercial sour	⅛ teaspoon almond extract
cream	¼ cup granulated sugar
2 egg yolks	Strawberry Glacé, below
2 tablespoons milk	

Early on day:
1. Make and bake pie shell; cool.
2. Sprinkle gelatin on water to soften. In saucepan combine sour cream, egg yolks, milk, 2 tablespoons sugar, and salt. Cook, over medium heat, stirring constantly, 5 minutes. Remove from heat, stir in softened gelatin. Refrigerate mixture, stirring occasionally, until thick and completely chilled, but not stiff.
3. With mixer at high speed, beat egg whites with almond extract until soft peaks form. Gradually beat in ¼ cup sugar, beating until stiff; then fold into gelatin mixture. Spoon into cooled pie shell; refrigerate.
4. Make Strawberry Glacé; spread evenly over top of pie; refrigerate again until firm—about 2 hours in all. Makes 8 servings.

STRAWBERRY GLACÉ: Thaw, then drain, reserving juice, 1 10-ounce package frozen sliced strawberries. In saucepan, add strawberry juice to 1 tablespoon cornstarch and few drops red food color. Cook, over medium heat, stirring constantly, until mixture is clear and thickened. Stir in strawberries.

SWISS WALNUT PIE
(Pictured opposite)

1½ cups granulated sugar	¼ teaspoon salt
2 cups chopped walnuts	¾ cup shortening
2 tablespoons liquid honey	⅓ cup granulated sugar
½ cup light cream	1 egg, beaten (reserve 1
2 cups sifted regular all-	tablespoon)
purpose flour	1 tablespoon water

Make up to 3 days ahead:
1. In large skillet, over medium heat, melt 1½ cups sugar, stirring constantly, until it forms a golden syrup. Add walnuts and honey; mix well; then stir in cream; let cool.

2.   In large bowl combine flour and salt. With pastry blender or 2 knives, cut in shortening until like corn meal. Add ⅓ cup sugar, egg, and water; mix well. Form into smooth ball; then, if kitchen is warm, wrap pastry in wax paper and refrigerate 30 minutes.

3.   Cut off and reserve one third of pastry. On lightly floured surface, roll rest of pastry into circle ¼ inch thick. Fold it in half, then lift onto ungreased 9-inch layer-cake pan; unfold and press gently to fit pan. Trim pastry even with top edge of layer-cake pan. Spread walnut mixture evenly over bottom; fold sides of pastry down over filling.

4.   Start heating oven to 350°F.

5.   Roll out reserved pastry. With an S-shaped cookie cutter 2¼ inches long (or any other small shaped cutter) cut out about 20 pastry shapes. Arrange around top edge of pie, slightly overlapping. Then criss-cross 2 more shapes in center of pie as pictured. Brush shapes with reserved beaten egg.

6.   Bake at 350°F. 20 minutes, then turn oven up to 375°F. and bake 20 minutes longer. Cool on wire rack.

7.   With spatula, loosen pie around edges. Place a plate over top of it; invert pie and plate together. Lift off pan; place serving plate lightly on bottom of pie; invert both pie and plate to turn pie right side up. Refrigerate until serving time.

DATE-WALNUT PIE

1 unbaked 9-inch pie shell
½ cup light-brown sugar, packed
½ cup soft butter or margarine
¼ cup granulated sugar
3 eggs, unbeaten
¼ teaspoon salt
¼ cup corn syrup
½ cup milk or light cream
1 cup coarsely-chopped walnuts
½ teaspoon vanilla extract
1 cup cut-up pitted dates
1 cup heavy cream (optional)
8 pitted dates (optional)
Chopped walnuts (optional)

Make day before, if desired:

1.   Prepare pie shell with fluted edge.

2.   Start heating oven to 350°F.

3.   In double-boiler top mix brown sugar and butter until well blended. Add granulated sugar; mix well. Add eggs, one at a time, beating well after each addition, to blend. Add salt, corn syrup, and milk; mix well. Cook, over boiling water, stirring constantly, 5 minutes. Remove from water; stir in 1 cup chopped nuts, vanilla, and cut-up dates. Pour into pie shell.

4.   Bake 1 hour; cool; refrigerate.

At serving time:

Whip cream. Place spoonfuls, in ring, around top of pie. Arrange whole dates on whipped cream; sprinkle with a few chopped nuts. Makes 8 servings.

Swiss Walnut Pie

Coconut Apricot Chiffon P

Here are "glamour" crusts that can make an ordinary pie into an elegant, extra-special pie in minutes.

BAKED CRUMB CRUSTS

Kind of crumbs (use 1⅓ cups):	Granulated sugar:	Butter or margarine:
Graham crackers—16	¼ cup	¼ cup
Vanilla wafers—24 (2")	none	¼ cup
Chocolate wafers —18 (2¾")	none	3 tablespoons
Gingersnaps—20 (2")	none	6 tablespoons
Corn or wheat flakes—3 cups	2 tablespoons	¼ cup

1. Start heating oven to 375°F.
2. Let butter soften. Place long piece wax paper on pastry board; stack choice of crackers or cookies, or pour cereal, along center. Wrap, making double fold in paper; tuck ends under. Roll fine with rolling pin. Or roll out in plastic bag.
3. In 2-cup measuring cup, with fork, mix 1⅓ cups crumbs, sugar (if any), and butter until crumbly. Set aside 3 tablespoons of this mixture. With back of spoon, press rest to bottom and sides of 9-inch pie plate, forming small rim.
4. Bake 8 minutes; cool; fill as recipe directs; top with reserved crumbs.

NUT-CRUMB CRUST: Reduce quantity of crumbs to 1 cup; add ½ cup finely-chopped walnuts, pecans, almonds, or Brazil nuts.

MARBLE CRUMB CRUST: Reduce quantity of crumbs to 1 cup. Add 2 squares unsweetened chocolate, grated.

UNBAKED CRUMB CRUSTS

Pretzel Crust

Packaged pretzel sticks
¼ cup soft butter or margarine

3 tablespoons granulated sugar

1. With rolling pin, crush enough pretzel sticks to make ¾ cup *coarse* crumbs.
2. In 9-inch pie plate, blend crumbs with butter and sugar. Press to bottom and sides of pie plate; refrigerate until well chilled, then fill as recipe directs.

Graham Cracker Crust

1⅓ cups graham-cracker crumbs
⅓ cup brown sugar, packed

½ teaspoon cinnamon
⅓ cup melted butter or margarine

1. Prepare crumbs as in step 2 of Baked Crumb Crusts.
2. Mix crumbs, brown sugar, cinnamon, and butter until crumbly. Set aside 3 tablespoons of this mixture. With back of spoon, press rest to bottom and sides of well-greased 9-inch pie plate; *do not spread on rim.* Refrigerate until well chilled. Fill as recipe directs; sprinkle with reserved crumbs. Refrigerate.
Note: Graham-cracker crumbs come finely rolled in a 13¾-ounce package—ample for 3 9-inch pie shells.

NUT AND COCONUT CRUSTS

Nut Crust

1 cup finely-ground Brazil nuts, pecans, walnuts, blanched almonds, or peanuts

2 tablespoons granulated sugar

1. Start heating oven to 400°F.
2. Mix nuts with sugar. With back of spoon, press to bottom and sides of 8- or 9-inch pie plate; *do not spread on rim.*
3. Bake about 8 minutes; cool. Fill as recipe directs.

Toasted-Nut Crust

1½ cups Brazil nuts, walnuts, or pecans
¼ cup granulated sugar

⅛ teaspoon salt
1 egg white

1. Start heating oven to 375°F. Butter 9-inch pie plate; then line bottom with wax paper; butter paper.
2. With medium blade of food grinder, grind nuts. Mix with sugar and salt. Beat egg white until soft peaks form; blend into nut mixture. Press firmly to bottom and sides (not rim) of prepared pie plate.
3. Bake 12 to 15 minutes, or until light brown. With small spatula, carefully loosen around side; let stand 10 minutes.
4. Lift crust to slip out wax paper; let cool. Fill as recipe directs.

Toasted-Coconut Crust

2 tablespoons soft butter or margarine

1½ cups flaked coconut

1. Start heating oven to 300°F.
2. Spread butter evenly in 8- or 9-inch pie plate. Pat coconut evenly onto butter.
3. Bake 15 to 20 minutes, or until golden; cool. Fill as recipe directs.

Unbaked Coconut Crust

1½ cups fine-grated coconut
½ cup confectioners' sugar

3 tablespoons melted butter or margarine

1. Combine coconut with confectioners' sugar. Gradually stir in melted butter.
2. Press coconut mixture evenly over bottom and sides of oiled 8- or 9-inch pie plate. Refrigerate until firm. Fill as recipe directs.

COCONUT APRICOT CHIFFON PIE
(Pictured on page 22)

2½ cups flaked coconut
7 tablespoons melted butter
 or margarine
1 1-pound 14-ounce can
 whole unpeeled apricots

2 envelopes unflavored
 gelatin
1 12-ounce can apricot
 nectar
¼ cup lemon juice
3 egg whites, unbeaten

Early on day:

1. Start heating oven to 300°F.
2. In bowl toss coconut with butter until well blended. In layer-cake pan spread ⅓ cup coconut mixture; with fork, press remaining coconut mixture to bottom, sides, and rim of 9-inch pie plate.
3. Bake both until crust is light golden and coconut in cake pan is toasted—about 20 minutes; cool.
4. Drain whole apricots, reserving juice. Cut apricots in half; refrigerate.
5. Onto ½ cup apricot juice, in 2-quart bowl, sprinkle gelatin. Heat apricot nectar to boiling; add to softened gelatin mixture, stirring until gelatin is completely dissolved. Then stir in remaining apricot juice and lemon juice; refrigerate until mixture is stiff enough to mound when dropped from spoon—about 1 hour and 15 to 30 minutes—stirring occasionally after first hour.
6. Now to chilled gelatin mixture add unbeaten egg whites; with mixer at high speed, beat until light, fluffy, and a delicate apricot color. Refrigerate until stiff enough to hold shape.
7. Now with rubber spatula or spoon, fold syrup at bottom of bowl into apricot mixture until *just* blended. Then spoon into cooled coconut crust. Refrigerate 30 minutes.
8. Then, on top, arrange 12 apricot halves in pairs as pictured; refrigerate until served — at least 3 hours and 30 minutes.

Just before serving:
Garnish top of pie with small mounds of toasted coconut. Pass rest of apricot halves, if desired. Makes 8 servings.

MOCHA PIE

1 7¼-ounce package
 vanilla wafers
¼ cup soft butter or
 margarine
1 envelope unflavored
 gelatin
¼ cup cold water
½ cup cocoa

½ cup granulated sugar
½ teaspoon salt
2 teaspoons instant coffee
 powder
¾ cup boiling water
4 egg yolks, slightly beaten
4 egg whites
½ pint heavy cream

Make day before:

1. With rolling pin or electric blender, finely crush enough vanilla wafers to make 1⅓ cups crumbs (about

24). Then, with fork, in 9-inch pie plate blend crumbs and butter well. Press mixture to bottom and sides of pie plate, lining it evenly; refrigerate.
2. Soften gelatin in cold water; stir over hot water until dissolved; set aside.
3. In double boiler combine cocoa, sugar, salt, and instant coffee powder. Gradually add boiling water, stirring with wire whip or metal spoon; continue stirring until smooth. Now, over hot, *not boiling*, water, stir in egg yolks; cook, stirring constantly, until thickened. Remove from heat; stir in gelatin. Turn into large bowl; refrigerate until chilled, but not set, stirring once or twice.
4. Meanwhile, beat egg whites until stiff enough to hold soft peaks; then whip ½ cup cream. At one time, fold both into well-chilled chocolate mixture. Pour into cooled crust; refrigerate.

Just before serving:
Whip remaining heavy cream; spread over top of pie. Makes 8 servings.

BLACK-BOTTOM PIE
(Pictured opposite)

1 Baked Gingersnap-Crumb
 Crust, page 23
1 package vanilla-pudding-
 and-pie-filling mix
1 envelope unflavored
 gelatin
2 egg yolks
1½ cups milk

2 squares unsweetened
 chocolate
3 egg whites
Pinch cream of tartar
¼ cup granulated sugar
2 tablespoons rum
½ cup heavy cream,
 whipped
9 gingersnap halves

Early on day:

1. Prepare baked crumb crust as directed, using an 8-inch pie plate; cool.
2. Mix pudding mix with gelatin. Beat egg yolks with milk. Stir into pudding mixture in saucepan. Cook, over low heat, stirring, until thickened and almost starting to boil.
3. Melt 1½ squares chocolate in double-boiler top, over hot, *not boiling,* water. Stir in half of pudding mixture until smooth; spoon into cooled crust. Refrigerate rest of pudding mixture until just beginning to set.
4. Meanwhile, beat egg whites with cream of tartar until moist peaks are formed when beater is raised. Add sugar gradually, beating until stiff. Then carefully fold in remaining pudding mixture and rum.
5. Pour as much of egg-white mixture on chocolate layer as pie shell will hold; refrigerate a few minutes, then pour rest on top. Refrigerate until set.
6. Now top with whipped cream. Insert gingersnap halves in cream as pictured; with vegetable parer, shave remaining ½ square chocolate over top; refrigerate until served. Makes 8 servings.

Orange Confetti Pie

Black-Bottom Pie

ORANGE CONFETTI PIE
(Pictured on page 25)

1 Baked Graham-Cracker-
  Crumb Crust, page 23
1 3-ounce package lemon-
  flavor gelatin
1 3-ounce package orange-
  flavor gelatin

3 cups boiling water
1 envelope unflavored
  gelatin
½ cup orange juice
2 oranges
1½ cups heavy cream

Early on day:
1. Prepare baked crumb crust as directed; cool.
2. Make up lemon- and orange-flavor gelatin as package labels direct, using 1½ cups boiling water for each package. Pour each into 8-inch layer-cake pan; refrigerate until set.
3. Sprinkle unflavored gelatin on orange juice to soften; then, stir, over hot water, until dissolved. Refrigerate until consistency of unbeaten egg white.
4. Peel and section oranges, then cut into bite-size pieces; add to unflavored gelatin mixture. Now beat 1 cup cream until stiff; fold into gelatin mixture.
5. Cut firm lemon- and orange-flavor gelatins into ¾-inch cubes. Fold half of cubes into whipped-cream mixture. Lightly pile into cooled crust. Refrigerate remaining cubes and pie for at least 3 hours, but not longer than 8 hours.

Just before serving:
Whip ½ cup cream until stiff; spread over top of pie. Scatter remaining lemon- and orange-flavor gelatin cubes over whipped cream leaving about 1-inch border of whipped cream. Makes 6 to 8 servings.

CHERRY-CHEESE PIE
(Pictured below)

2 cups packaged finely-
  crushed graham-cracker
  crumbs
⅓ cup granulated sugar
½ cup melted butter or
  margarine

1 package dessert-topping
  mix
1 8-ounce package cream
  cheese, softened
1 1-pound 5-ounce can
  cherry-pie filling

Make pie day before:
1. Start heating oven to 375°F.
2. In bowl combine crumbs and sugar; with fork, mix in butter until mixture is crumbly. Press mixture to bottom and sides of 10-inch pie plate.
3. Bake about 10 minutes, or until golden; cool.
4. In small bowl make up dessert-topping mix as package label directs; then with mixer, beat in cream cheese. Pile lightly in cooled crust, just inside outer edge, making a ring about 2½ inches wide as pictured. Pour cherry filling into center of pie. Refrigerate.

Cherry-Cheese Pie

ORANGE-ANGEL PIE

1 Toasted-Coconut Crust, page 23	1 teaspoon grated orange peel
1 envelope unflavored gelatin	1 teaspoon grated lemon peel
Granulated sugar	3 egg whites
½ teaspoon salt	1 cup diced orange sections
3 egg yolks, slightly beaten	1 cup heavy cream
1 cup orange juice	1 orange

Early on day, or about 4 hours before serving:
1. Prepare baked Toasted-Coconut Crust as directed; cool.
2. In double boiler combine gelatin, ½ cup sugar, and salt; stir in egg yolks and orange juice. Cook, over hot, not boiling, water, stirring constantly, until slightly thickened. Stir in orange and lemon peels. Refrigerate until partially set, stirring occasionally.
3. Beat egg whites until soft peaks form; gradually beat in ⅓ cup sugar, beating until stiff. Fold into gelatin mixture; fold in diced orange sections, drained of juice. Refrigerate until mixture mounds when dropped from spoon. Pour into cooled crust; refrigerate until set—about 2 hours, or until needed.

Just before serving:
Whip cream; top pie with mounds of cream; garnish with orange, in sections. Makes 8 servings.

PEACHY CREAM-CHEESE PIE

1 Unbaked Graham-Cracker-Crumb Crust, page 23	½ teaspoon vanilla extract
1½ 8-ounce packages cream cheese	1 1-pound 13-ounce can sliced peaches
2 eggs, unbeaten	¼ cup apricot preserves
½ cup granulated sugar	1 teaspoon lemon juice

Day before, or early on day:
1. Prepare mixture for crumb crust as directed; press firmly to bottom and sides of 8-inch pie plate; refrigerate.
2. Start heating oven to 350°F.
3. In medium bowl, with mixer at medium speed, beat cream cheese, eggs, sugar, and vanilla until smooth, scraping bowl and beaters as needed. Pour this mixture into chilled crust.
4. Bake 30 minutes, or until set; cool on wire rack.
5. Meanwhile, drain peach slices; then carefully split each slice lengthwise in half. Place these thin slices on paper-towel-covered cookie sheet; cover with paper towel, then pat dry. Refrigerate on cookie sheet.
6. When pie is cool, start at outer edge to arrange peach slices, petal fashion, in overlapping rows over top.
7. In small saucepan, melt apricot preserves; stir in lemon juice. Brush apricot mixture over peach slices; refrigerate until served. Makes 8 servings.

Pastries

CONTINENTAL CHEESE SWIRLS

2 cups sifted regular all-purpose flour	Grated peel of 1 lemon
Salt	Granulated sugar
Salad oil	¼ teaspoon cinnamon
½ cup warm water	⅔ cup light raisins, packed
3 8-ounce packages small-curd cottage cheese	2 egg yolks
1 egg, beaten	1 teaspoon light cream
1½ tablespoons flour	Commercial sour cream
	Raspberry sauce or apple-sauce

Make, then freeze several days ahead, or make early on serving day:
1. Into large bowl sift 2 cups flour with ¼ teaspoon salt. Stir in ¼ cup salad oil and water. With floured, plastic gloves on hands, knead dough in bowl until blended and soft. Then brush dough with salad oil; cover with towel; set in warm place for 1 hour.
2. Press cottage cheese through food mill or strainer into bowl. Add egg, 1½ tablespoons flour, lemon peel, 3 tablespoons sugar, cinnamon, ½ teaspoon salt, and raisins. Blend well; set aside.
3. Cut dough into thirds. On lightly floured, cloth-covered surface, roll out one third about ⅛ inch thick (keep rest covered in bowl). Slip back of hand under dough and lift off surface, shifting hands and dough as needed until it is stretched evenly, almost paper thin. Now lower dough so it rests on surface; then, with fingers gently pull edges to paper thinness all over, and into an 18-inch square. Cut square, parallel to bottom edge, into 3 equal strips, each 6 inches wide.
4. One inch in from edge of one strip spread 4½ tablespoons cheese mixture in row 1-inch wide. Now, while lifting cloth, roll strip of dough over filling, jelly-roll fashion. Move roll away from other strips, turning seam side down; then gently coil it loosely into a swirl, tucking end under. Lift with broad spatula to greased jelly-roll pan.
5. Repeat step 4 with other two strips; then repeat steps 3 and 4 with remaining two-thirds of dough, arranging swirls in two pans. Cover with foil; refrigerate or freeze.

About 1 hour before serving:
1. Start heating oven to 375°F.
2. Remove pans from refrigerator or freezer; unwrap. Brush swirls with egg yolks blended with cream.
3. Bake 40 minutes, or until golden; remove from oven; sprinkle with granulated sugar.

28

4. Serve warm; pass sour cream and/or one of sauces. Makes 9 servings.

CARAMEL APPLE DUMPLINGS
(Pictured opposite)

1 package piecrust mix	2 tablespoons butter or
3 medium baking apples	margarine
1 egg, beaten	⅓ cup dark-brown sugar
½ cup caramel sauce	¾ cup water
(from a jar)	¼ cup canned toasted
	slivered almonds

About 1 hour and 30 minutes before serving:
1. Prepare piecrust mix as package label directs; roll out ⅛ inch thick. With pastry wheel cut out 3 7-inch squares, 6 strips, 6 inches long and ¾ inch wide, and 3 1-inch circles, rerolling dough as needed.
2. Start heating oven to 350°F.
3. Wash, pare, and core apples; place one on each of 7-inch squares. Turn all four points of dough up to top of each apple, forming 4 "ears," pressing edges lightly together. Now, over each dumpling lay 2 strips of dough crosswise, then top with a pastry circle.
4. Brush dumplings with egg, then place in medium, shallow baking dish. In small saucepan combine caramel sauce, butter, brown sugar, and water; bring to boil, stirring, then pour over dumplings.
5. Bake 40 minutes, or until apples are just tender, spooning caramel sauce over them occasionally.
6. Just before serving, sprinkle almonds over dumplings. Makes 3 servings.

WIKIWIKIS
(Dessert Pizzas)

Favorite pastry (or pack-	One of fillings, below
aged piecrust mix) for	
9-inch pie shell	

1. Start heating oven to 450°F.
2. Make up pastry; roll out to ⅛ inch thickness; use to line 9-inch foil pizza pan or layer-cake pan (if cake pan is used, extend crust ½ inch up sides). Prick well with fork.
3. Bake 10 minutes, or until lightly browned.
4. Meanwhile, set out ingredients for desired filling; in baked crust layer filling as directed. Turn oven temperature down to 425°F.
5. Bake pizza about 10 minutes, or until coconut is golden. Cut into wedges and serve warm. Makes 6 to 8 servings.

Fillings (choose any one)

PRUNE AND APRICOT: Mix ½ cup commercial sour cream (or 2 3-ounce packages soft cream cheese) with ⅛ teaspoon cinnamon, dash nutmeg, and 2 tablespoons confectioners' sugar. Layer this mixture with ½ cup pitted well-cooked prunes combined with ½ cup cooked dried apricots; then top with ½ cup packaged fine-grated coconut.

CINNAMON APPLESAUCE: Layer 1 cup tart applesauce (tinted delicate pink with red food color) with 1 tablespoon red cinnamon candies and 2 tablespoons chopped walnuts; then top with ½ cup packaged fine-grated coconut, and sprinkle with cinnamon.

CREAM-CHEESE PRESERVES: Layer 2 3-ounce packages soft cream cheese with ¼ cup strawberry or apricot preserves and 2 tablespoons chopped walnuts; then top with ½ cup packaged fine-grated coconut.

APPLE CHEESE: Layer 1 cup grated Cheddar cheese with 1½ cups canned apple-pie filling, then ¼ cup currants or raisins; now top with ½ cup packaged fine-grated coconut; sprinkle with cinnamon.

MINTED-CHEESE PINEAPPLE: Layer 2 3-ounce packages cream cheese softened with a little pineapple juice, with 1 8¾-ounce can crushed pineapple (drained, then flavored with a few drops mint extract); top with ½ cup packaged fine-grated coconut.

FRENCH PUFF PASTRIES: Puff Paste
(Pictured on page 30)

3½ cups sifted regular	1 pound chilled, but not
all-purpose flour	hard, butter or
1 cup ice water	margarine (4 sticks)

Any time up to 1 month ahead, make Puff Paste, shape pastries, and freeze them:
1. Into medium bowl sift flour. Add ice water in small amounts, mixing thoroughly with fork to form a stiff dough. On unfloured surface, knead dough 5 minutes, then flour surface and set dough on it under the bowl. Let stand 15 minutes.
2. Then, on floured surface, roll dough into rectangle ¼-inch thick, turning it over frequently to keep edges straight. Quickly spread two thirds of dough with 1 stick butter. Fold unbuttered third over top of middle third, then fold remaining third over top to form 3 layers, with all edges meeting *exactly*. This completes the first "turn." Repeat, keeping folded edge toward you while rolling.
3. Now wrap folded dough in 1 layer of wax paper and place directly on freezer shelf or bottom for 10 minutes, turning over at end of 5 minutes.
4. Then, using last 2 sticks butter, repeat steps 2 and 3, for a total of 4 "turns." Now roll and fold enough twice more, omitting butter, for a total of 6 "turns." Wrap dough in foil; refrigerate overnight.
Next day:
Roll out, cut, and shape pastries, then freeze as recipes direct. If making more than one kind of pastry, divide Puff Paste in half, thirds, or quarters before shaping each portion.

Caramel Apple Dumplings

RASPBERRY PUFFS

Puff Paste, page 28   Raspberry jam
Confectioners' sugar

Day after Puff Paste is made:

1.   On floured surface, roll out Puff Paste ¼ inch thick. Cut into 1¾- or 2-inch rounds. Then, with one light stroke of rolling pin, form each into oval.

2.   With ½-inch-round cookie cutter, score center of each oval, cutting almost, but not quite, through. Foil-wrap; place side by side, not stacked, on cookie sheet; freeze until needed.

Early on serving day:

1.   Start heating oven to 450°F.

2.   Place frozen ovals, 2½ inches apart, on brown-paper-lined cookie sheet.

3.   Bake 5 minutes; then, every 5 minutes, turn oven down 50 degrees, until ovals are puffed and golden— about 10 minutes—15 minutes in all. Cool on rack.

4.   With sharp knife, remove centers of puffs along with bit of pastry underneath; sprinkle with confectioners' sugar; fill centers with jam. Makes about 50.

PALM LEAVES

Puff Paste, page 28   Granulated sugar

Day after Puff Paste is made:

1.   On sugared surface, roll Puff Paste ½ inch thick; sprinkle with sugar, turn over and roll into rectangle three times as long as it is wide and ⅜ inch thick. Sprinkle with ¼ cup sugar.

2.   Folds ends of dough to meet in center; flatten slightly; now fold folded edges in again to meet in center; flatten slightly. Fold in half lengthwise. Press roll firmly together; refrigerate 1 hour. Cut into 3 equal portions; wrap each in wax paper, then foil; freeze until needed.

Early on serving day:

1.   Let rolls stand, unwrapped, at room temperature 45 minutes. Then turn each roll on its side and cut into ⅜-inch slices. Arrange, 3 inches apart, on brown-paper-lined cookie sheet; refrigerate 15 minutes.

2.   Meanwhile, start heating oven to 450°F.

3.   Bake 5 minutes; now quickly turn over, spreading ends slightly apart with spatula. Reduce oven heat to 350°F. Bake 15 to 20 minutes, or until golden and crisp. Cool on wire rack. Makes about 3½ dozen.

CREAM-FILLED SHELLS

Puff Paste, page 28   ¼ cup light rum (optional)
1 package vanilla- or   ½ cup heavy cream,
   chocolate-pudding-and-   whipped
   pie-filling mix

Day after Puff Paste is made:

On floured surface, roll half of Puff Paste ⅜ inch thick. Cut into about 15 2¾-inch rounds; foil-wrap; place side by side, not stacked, on cookie sheet; freeze until needed.

French Puff Pastries

Repeat with other half of Puff Paste.

Early on serving day:
1. Start heating oven to 450°F.
2. Lay frozen rounds, 3 inches apart, on large brown-paper-lined cookie sheet.
3. Bake 10 minutes; then, every 5 minutes, turn oven down 50 degrees, until rounds are puffed and golden—about 15 minutes—25 minutes in all. Cool on rack.
4. Meanwhile, using 1½ cups milk, prepare pudding mix as package label directs. Stir in rum; lay wax paper directly on surface; refrigerate until very cold.
5. Beat pudding until smooth; fold in whipped cream; refrigerate.

About 1 hour before serving:
With very sharp knife, split each pastry shell into 2 or 3 layers; spread 1 to 2 tablespoons pudding over each layer. If desired, decorate top of each with whipped cream rosette. Refrigerate. Makes about 30.

CREAM HORNS

¼ of Puff Paste, page 28
1 egg white, beaten
½ pint heavy cream
¼ cup confectioners' sugar
1 teaspoon vanilla extract

Day after Puff Paste is made:
1. Prepare foil cone forms: Cut doubled heavy-duty foil into 12 8-inch squares. Fold each square to make a triangle, then roll to a cone shape, folding its top over wide end, to make cone firm.
2. Remove one fourth of Puff Paste from refrigerator. On floured surface, roll out paper-thin; cut into 12 strips ¾ to 1 inch wide, 13 to 14 inches long. Starting 1 inch above small end of foil cone, spiral one of strips, letting each row overlap next ⅛ to ¼ inch; do not extend dough over wide end of cone. Moisten end, then pinch firmly to anchor strip to cone. Repeat with rest of cones.
3. Refrigerate cones 15 minutes, then wrap individually in foil and freeze until needed.

Early on serving day:
1. Start heating oven to 450°F.
2. Combine egg white with 2 tablespoons water. Unwrap cones. Lay, seam side down, 2 inches apart, on brown-paper-lined cookie sheet. With fingers, firmly press cones to paper. Brush tops with egg white.
3. Bake 5 or 6 minutes, or until puffed and golden; turn heat down to 350°F. Bake 5 to 8 minutes longer. Carefully remove foil cones; return horns to oven 3 to 5 minutes to dry out. Cool on wire rack.

About 1 hour before serving:
Whip cream with confectioners' sugar and vanilla; using decorating bag with number 5 tube, press whipped cream into each horn, ending with a swirl. If desired, sprinkle swirls with chopped nuts or shaved chocolate. Refrigerate at least 30 minutes. Makes 12 servings.

BLENDER DESSERT PANCAKES

1 cup orange juice
¼ cup milk
3 tablespoons salad oil
1 egg, unbeaten
3 tablespoons granulated sugar
¾ teaspoon salt
1¼ cups sifted regular all-purpose flour
2½ teaspoons double-acting baking powder
Brandied Strawberry Sauce, below

1. Place all ingredients except sauce in electric-blender container. Cover and blend at high speed for about 20 seconds, or until smooth. (Stop blender once or twice and scrape down sides with rubber spatula.)
2. Pour some of batter onto lightly greased hot griddle, making pancakes about 4 inches in diameter. Cook until golden on one side; turn; cook until done. Roll up and keep warm. Repeat, using rest of batter.
3. Serve topped with Brandied Strawberry Sauce; pass remaining sauce. Makes 12.

BRANDIED STRAWBERRY SAUCE: Drain 1 10-ounce package frozen sliced strawberries; thawed; set aside. Place another package thawed strawberries, 5 teaspoons cornstarch, and ½ cup red currant jelly in electric-blender container. Cover and blend at high speed about 1 minute. (Stop blender once or twice and scrape down sides with rubber spatula.) Pour into saucepan. Cook, stirring, over low heat, until thickened and clear. Stir in enough red food color to make bright red. Add ¼ cup brandy and drained strawberries. Keep warm over hot water while making Dessert Pancakes. Makes about 2¼ cups.

CRÊPES SUZETTE
(Pictured on page 33)

2 eggs, unbeaten
½ cup sifted regular all-purpose flour
1 tablespoon salad oil
¼ teaspoon salt
1 teaspoon granulated sugar
⅔ cup milk
6 sugar tablets or 12 cubes
1 orange
¼ cup orange juice
¼ cup butter or margarine
¼ cup curaçao or Cointreau
Orange twists
¼ cup Grand Marnier or brandy

Day before, or early on day:
1. In medium bowl, with hand beater, or mixer at medium speed, beat eggs; beat in flour until blended, then salad oil, salt, sugar, and milk, beating until smooth.
2. Lightly grease small skillet (about 5 or 6 inches

across), then heat until a drop of water "dances" on bottom. Pour about 2 tablespoons batter in skillet, then quickly rotate skillet to cover bottom with batter; cook, turning once, until lightly browned on both sides. Remove and keep warm, while repeating with remaining batter, making and stacking at least 10 crêpes. Wrap in foil or saran; refrigerate.

3. Rub sugar tablets over orange to absorb some oil and peel. In small saucepan combine tablets with orange juice, butter, and curaçao. Heat until butter melts and sugar is dissolved. Pour into small bowl; cover and refrigerate.

About 5 minutes before serving:

1. In crêpe pan of chafing dish, over medium heat, reheat orange sauce until butter is melted. Fold crêpes in quarters; place in sauce to reheat, spooning on sauce. Add orange twist.

2. With crêpe pan over small flame, pour Grand Marnier gently over sauce. Heat, without stirring, but do not boil. Ignite with match. When flame dies, serve crêpes with sauce. Makes 4 or 5 servings.

SWEDISH PANCAKES
(Pictured opposite)

1 cup sifted regular all-purpose flour	2 tablespoons melted butter or margarine
2 tablespoons granulated sugar	Few drops vanilla extract
½ teaspoon salt	Butter, margarine, or shortening
3 eggs, unbeaten	Lingonberry preserves
3 cups milk	Sweetened whipped cream (optional)

About 2 hours before serving:

Sift flour with sugar and salt. In large bowl with hand beater, slightly beat eggs; add milk, melted butter, and vanilla, beating just until well blended. Add flour mixture, all at once, beating until well blended; refrigerate.

At serving time:

1. Start heating plätt pan; brush with butter. (If you don't have a platt pan, fold 3-inch-wide strips of foil lengthwise in half twice; form into about 7 3-inch circles, fastening ends together with paper clips or staples. Set on greased, heated griddle.)

2. Remove batter from refrigerator; beat slightly. When plätt pan is very hot, pour about 1 tablespoon batter into each section (or into each foil circle); cook until top is covered with tiny bubbles and underside is *well browned.* Then, with 2 small spatulas, turn each pancake, and brown other side; keep warm while making rest of pancakes.

3. To serve, arrange pancakes on heated platter or individual plates in stacks, of 7 or 8, or in overlapping circles. Pass lingonberry preserves and whipped cream. Makes 10 servings.

CHERRY-BERRY CREPES
(Pictured opposite)

4 eggs	Grated peel of 1 lemon
Salt	2 8-ounce packages small-curd cottage cheese
Granulated sugar	¼ teaspoon cinnamon
1½ cups water	1 teaspoon farina or flour
1½ cups sifted regular all-purpose flour	Blueberry Sauce, below
½ teaspoon double-acting baking powder	Berry-Cherry Sauce, below
Butter or margarine	Commercial sour cream

Make and fill crepes up to 1 week ahead and freeze, or make day before and refrigerate.

1. With mixer at medium speed, beat 3 eggs; then gradually beat in ¾ teaspoon salt, 1½ teaspoons sugar, water, then flour sifted with baking powder.

2. Lightly brush medium-hot 5½-inch skillet with butter; quickly pour in enough batter, while tipping skillet, to *thinly* coat bottom of skillet (about 2 tablespoons); quickly pour excess into cup. Cook crepe until dry on top and slightly brown on bottom. Turn out on paper towel to cool. Repeat, brushing skillet with butter as needed. When cool, stack crepes carefully; wrap in wax paper.

3. Make filling: Place grated lemon peel in bowl; press cottage cheese through food mill or strainer into same bowl. Stir in 1 egg, beaten, 1 tablespoon sugar, ¼ teaspoon salt, cinnamon, and farina.

4. Place a heaping tablespoon of this mixture at edge of one of crepes; roll up jelly-roll fashion. Repeat. Lay filled crepes, side by side, seam side down, on flat baking pan. Cover with foil; freeze or refrigerate until ready to serve.

Early on serving day:

Prepare Blueberry and Berry-Cherry Sauces as directed.

Just before serving:

1. Remove crepes from freezer or refrigerator; unwrap, but do not thaw. In melted butter, in large skillet, brown crepes, first on seam side, then on other side, turning carefully.

2. Serve on platter, topped with sour cream and some of each sauce. Pass rest of sauces and sour cream. Makes 9 servings of 2 crepes each.

BLUEBERRY SAUCE: In saucepan blend 1 tablespoon cornstarch and 2 tablespoons granulated sugar. Add juice drained from 1 10-ounce package frozen blueberries, thawed. Stir over medium heat until clear and thickened. Stir in blueberries, then heat through. Cool.

BERRY-CHERRY SAUCE: Press 1 10-ounce package frozen sliced strawberries, thawed, through sieve. Blend 1 tablespoon cornstarch with 1 tablespoon granulated sugar in saucepan; add strawberries. Stir, over medium heat, until thickened. Fold in ⅔ cup drained, canned sour pitted cherries in heavy syrup. Cool.

Crêpes Suzette

Cherry-Berry Crepes

Swedish Pancakes

34

Caramel-Custard Mold

White Mountain Pudding

Custards & Puddings

KITCHENETTE CARAMEL PUDDING

1 cup dark-brown sugar, packed	3 eggs, unbeaten
	1 cup milk
3 slices buttered fresh white or raisin bread, cut into ½-inch squares	Dash salt
	½ teaspoon vanilla extract
	Ice cream or whipped cream

1. Generously butter inside of double-boiler top; pour in brown sugar; then add bread squares.
2. Beat eggs with milk, salt, and vanilla; pour over bread; *do not stir.* Cook, over boiling water, covered, 1 hour.
3. Serve warm, with ice cream or whipped cream. Makes 4 servings.

KITCHENETTE CHOCOLATE PUDDING: Melt 1 square unsweetened chocolate in buttered double-boiler top; stir in brown sugar and ¼ cup milk. Stir over boiling water until sugar dissolves. Add bread, then eggs beaten with remaining milk, salt, and vanilla; *do not stir.* Cook as above.

CARAMEL-CUSTARD MOLD
(Pictured opposite)

1½ cups granulated sugar	2 teaspoons almond extract
6½ cups milk	¾ cup heavy cream
9 eggs	½ cup sliced blanched almonds
5 egg yolks	
¾ teaspoon salt	

Day before:
1. Place 1 cup sugar in heavy 10-inch skillet; shake so sugar is level. Place over high heat and watch for sugar to begin melting. Then immediately tilt pan back and forth slowly to keep sugar moving. By the time sugar has completely melted, it will be a light, golden brown. Remove from heat at once, and carefully pour into bottom of 2½-quart heatproof soufflé dish (in cold weather, first heat dish with hot water to prevent its cracking).
2. Start heating oven to 325°F.
3. In 6-quart kettle, scald milk. Meanwhile, place eggs and egg yolks in large bowl; add ½ cup sugar; with mixer at medium speed, beat until completely blended.
4. Pour eggs, all at once, stirring constantly, into scalded milk; add salt and almond extract. Set soufflé dish in small roasting pan; place on oven rack; fill pan with boiling water to within ½ inch of top. Remove 1 cup custard mixture; pour rest into soufflé dish; carefully pour in reserved custard.

5. Bake 1 hour and 20 minutes, or until silver knife, inserted in center, comes out clean. Remove soufflé dish at once from water; cool slightly on wire rack. Refrigerate overnight.

At serving time:
1. Run small spatula all around custard. Place rimmed serving plate upside down on top; invert; lift off soufflé dish (caramel will collect around custard).
2. Whip cream; spoon ¼ cup caramel syrup from around custard; fold into cream. Surround custard with almonds as pictured; pass whipped-cream sauce. Makes 12 servings.

SEMISWEET-COFFEE CUSTARDS

1¼ cups milk	1 egg, unbeaten
¼ cup granulated sugar	1 teaspoon vanilla extract
⅛ teaspoon salt	Coffee-flavored whipped cream (optional)
1 6-ounce package semi-sweet-chocolate pieces	

1. In saucepan combine ¼ cup milk, sugar, and salt; bring to boil; remove from heat. Add chocolate pieces; stir briskly until melted and smooth. With hand beater, beat in egg and vanilla. Gradually stir in remaining 1 cup milk.
2. Pour mixture into 4 ungreased 6-ounce custard cups; cover tightly with foil. Set cups in ½ inch hot water in 10- or 12-inch skillet. Then cover with lid or foil; simmer gently 30 minutes.
3. Serve warm, right from cups; or refrigerate until chilled, then unmold. Top with coffee-flavored whipped cream, if desired. Makes 4 servings.

BRAZILIAN COFFEE CUSTARDS

3 cups milk	½ cup granulated sugar
1 cup light cream	1 teaspoon vanilla extract
6 to 8 tablespoons instant coffee powder	1 teaspoon almond extract
	½ teaspoon salt
2 teaspoons grated orange peel	Nutmeg
	1 cup chopped Brazil nuts
4 eggs	1 egg white
1 egg yolk	3 tablespoons guava jelly

1. Start heating oven to 325°F.
2. In saucepan scald milk with cream; add coffee powder and orange peel; stir until well blended; cool 10 minutes.
3. Meanwhile, in small bowl, with mixer at low speed, slightly beat eggs with egg yolk and sugar. Now slowly add coffee mixture, then extracts and salt; blend well. Strain through fine strainer. Pour into 6 custard cups; sprinkle each with nutmeg. Set cups in shallow baking pan; fill pan with cold water to within ¾ inch from top of cups.
4. Bake 1 hour, or until silver knife, inserted in center,

comes out clean. Remove custards from water; cool; refrigerate.

Just before serving:

1. With small spatula, remove each custard from cup; arrange, upside down, on serving dish. Sprinkle with chopped nuts.
2. Beat egg white until quite stiff; then beat in jelly until stiff. Swirl over nut-topped custards. Makes 6 servings.

FLOATING PEACHES À LA NEIGE

2 egg yolks	3 or 4 canned cling-peach
1 teaspoon cornstarch	halves
3 tablespoons granulated	2 egg whites
sugar	2 tablespoons granulated
1½ cups milk	sugar
½ teaspoon vanilla extract	½ teaspoon vanilla extract
	Slivered almonds

Day before, or early on day:

1. In double-boiler combine egg yolks, cornstarch, 3 tablespoons sugar, and milk. Cook, over boiling water, stirring constantly, until thickened. Stir in ½ teaspoon vanilla; cool.
2. Place peach halves in glass serving dish; pour custard over them; refrigerate.

Just before serving:

Beat egg whites until they peak; beat in 2 tablespoons sugar and ½ teaspoon vanilla. Spoon, in small mounds, over custard around peaches; sprinkle with almonds. Makes 3 or 4 servings.

WHITE MOUNTAIN PUDDING
(Pictured on page 34)

2 quarts milk	¼ cup granulated sugar
1 cup farina	¼ cup cornstarch
1 cup granulated sugar	¼ teaspoon salt
1½ teaspoons salt	1 cup white corn syrup
½ teaspoon almond extract	2 teaspoons almond extract
2 teaspoons nutmeg	Red food color
1 1-pound 14-ounce can	Seedless green grapes
purple plums	

Day before:

In large kettle bring milk to boil. Gradually add farina, stirring constantly. Then stir in 1 cup sugar, 1½ teaspoons salt, and ½ teaspoon almond extract; sprinkle in nutmeg. Cook, over low heat, stirring constantly, 10 minutes, or until very thick. Pour mixture into well-greased 2-quart mold. Let mold set at room temperature until cool; then refrigerate.

Next day, about 30 minutes before serving:

1. Drain plums, reserving juice. In saucepan combine ¼ cup sugar, cornstarch, and ¼ teaspoon salt. Gradually stir in plum juice, plus water, if necessary, to make

2 cups. Then stir in corn syrup and 2 teaspoons almond extract. Cook, over low heat, stirring constantly, until clear and thickened. Then stir in few drops red food color to tint delicate pink.
2. Now set mold of pudding in hot water for 2 minutes; then invert serving plate over top of mold; invert both; carefully lift off mold. Garnish pudding with plums and tiny bunchlets of grapes as pictured. Spoon some of sauce over pudding; pass rest. Makes 10 to 12 servings.

FOR 5 OR 6: Halve all ingredients for pudding; make full amount of sauce, using extra sauce for topping another dessert next day.

PRUNE-RICE PUDDING

2½ to 3 cups pitted,	½ teaspoon salt
cooked prunes	¼ cup granulated sugar
2 teaspoons cinnamon	1 teaspoon vanilla extract
⅓ cup uncooked regular	3 egg yolks, slightly beaten
white rice	3 egg whites
2 cups milk, scalded	Pour cream

About 2 hours before serving:

1. Start heating oven to 350°F.
2. Arrange prunes with ⅓ cup of their juice over bottom of 1½-quart shallow baking dish; sprinkle with cinnamon.
3. In double boiler, over boiling water, cook rice with milk, salt, and sugar, covered, about 1 hour. Remove from heat; stir in vanilla and egg yolks.
4. Beat egg whites until stiff, but not dry; *partially* fold into rice mixture, leaving some egg-white fluffs still intact; spoon over prunes.
5. Bake 30 minutes. Serve warm, with cream. Makes 6 servings.

TOPAZ TAPIOCA

3 large apples, pared, cut	1 cup light-brown sugar,
into eighths	packed
2 tablespoons butter or	¾ teaspoon salt
margarine	2 tablespoons lemon juice
1 teaspoon mace	2¼ cups water
⅓ cup quick-cooking	Light cream
tapioca	

About 45 minutes before serving:

1. Start heating oven to 375°F.
2. Arrange apple slices, in even rows, slightly overlapping, in 9-by-9-by-2-inch baking dish. Dot with butter; sprinkle with mace.
3. In saucepan combine tapioca, brown sugar, salt, lemon juice, and water; bring to boil, stirring. Pour hot tapioca mixture over apple slices.
4. Bake 20 minutes. Serve hot or warm, with cream. Makes 6 servings.

Meringues

CRISP MERINGUE SHELLS

1 package fluffy-white- frosting mix	⅓ cup confectioners' sugar ⅓ cup cold water

Make any time from 2 days to 3 hours ahead:
1. Start heating oven to 275°F.
2. In small bowl, with mixer at low speed, beat frosting mix with confectioners' sugar and water until sugar is dissolved. Then beat, at high speed, until mixture holds very stiff peaks, scraping bowl ·and beaters as needed.
3. For each meringue shell, drop ⅓ cup mixture onto brown-paper-covered cookie sheet. Hollow out center to form shell.
4. Bake 45 minutes; then turn off oven heat and leave meringues in oven 45 minutes longer to dry out completely. Remove and let stand on cookie sheet 2 or 3 minutes; remove to wire rack to cool. Store, lightly covered with wax paper.
Just before serving:
Fill shells with ice cream, fruit, custard, or lemon filling. Top with whipped cream. Makes 8 shells.
CHEWY MERINGUE SHELLS: Start heating oven to 400°F. Make meringue shells as above; place in oven; close oven door quickly, then turn off heat. Leave in oven 5 hours or overnight without heat. (Don't peek!) Store and serve as above.

MERINGUES GLACÉES

6 egg whites	1 teaspoon vinegar
⅛ teaspoon salt	1 teaspoon vanilla extract
2 cups granulated sugar	

Day or so before serving:
1. Set egg whites out to come to room temperature—about 1 hour.
2. With mixer at high speed, beat egg whites with salt until stiff enough to hold shape. A low speed, add sugar, about 2 tablespoons at a time, beating about 2 minutes after each addition (this takes about 30 minutes).
3. Start heating oven to 275°F.
4. Add vinegar and vanilla to egg-white mixture; at high speed, beat 10 minutes longer. Drop by heaping spoonfuls onto buttered cookie sheet.
5. Bake 45 minutes; turn oven heat down to 250°F. and bake 15 minutes longer, or until creamy white and firm. Remove to wire rack; cool.
6. Cover meringues lightly with wax paper, saran, or

foil; store in covered container until needed—they keep well.
To serve:
Break each meringue apart like a biscuit. Fill lower part with ice cream or whipped cream; replace top; add spoonful of fruit or chocolate, butterscotch, or caramel sauce. Makes 18 to 24 shells.
MERINGUE NESTS: Prepare meringue mixture as directed above. Onto buttered cookie sheet, drop 1 teaspoon meringue; with spatula, spread into 2-inch circle. Repeat, making 7 circles, 2 inches apart, on each of 2 cookie sheets. Now, with remaining meringue in decorating bag, with number 3B tube in place, around top edge of circle press out a narrow collar of meringue; continue to press out 3 more round collars, keeping sides straight to form a nest. Repeat, making 14 nests. Bake and cool as directed. Store in covered container until needed. Makes 14 nests.

SCHAUM TORTE
(Pictured on page 38)

6 egg whites (¾ cup)	6 12-ounce packages frozen
⅛ teaspoon salt	sliced peaches, thawed
2 cups granulated sugar	at room temperature
1 teaspoon vinegar	3 cups heavy cream
½ teaspoon vanilla extract	2 tablespoons slivered
	toasted almonds

Day before:
1. Start heating oven to 275°F.
2. In large bowl, with mixer at high speed, beat egg whites with salt until frothy. Now add sugar, 2 tablespoons at a time, beating well after each addition. Then add vinegar and vanilla, and beat 10 minutes longer.
3. Meanwhile, cut 2 9-inch circles from brown paper; divide meringue mixture in half; spread half on each paper circle; place each circle on small cookie sheet.
4. Bake meringue layers 1 hour, or until firm. (Cracks are normal.) Cool on wire rack.
5. Repeat steps 1 through 4, making 4 layers in all. When cool, store in covered container.

Meringue Sundae

Schaum Torte

About 20 minutes before serving:
1. Thoroughly drain thawed peach slices; place side by side on paper towels.
2. Whip cream until stiff.
3. Place one meringue layer on serving plate; remove brown paper. Spread with one third whipped cream, top with one third peach slices. Repeat with 2 more layers, arranging peach slices on top layer as pictured. Sprinkle with almonds. (Store fourth layer in covered container for later use.)
4. Cut with long sharp knife into wedges. (Meringue will not cut evenly as does a cake.) Makes 12 to 16 servings.

MERINGUE SUNDAE
(Pictured opposite)

6 egg whites	2 pints fresh strawberries
½ teaspoon cream of tartar	1 pound frozen cherries
2 cups granulated sugar	2 bananas
About 20 strawberry ice-cream balls (5 pints)	Lemon juice
	Green leaves

Night before serving:
1. Start heating oven to 400°F.
2. In large bowl, with mixer at high speed, beat egg whites with cream of tartar until frothy. At low speed, beat in sugar, 2 tablespoons at a time, beating until dissolved. Then continue beating, at high speed, until very stiff and glossy.
3. Meanwhile, cover cookie sheet with brown paper. On paper, with spatula, spread meringue in rectangle about 15 by 11 inches; then build up sides so they are about 2 inches wide by spreading meringue from center to sides, thus forming a shell.
4. Place meringue in oven; turn off heat. Let shell stay in oven overnight. (Don't peek.) Next morning remove it.
Early on serving day:
1. Make ice-cream balls, using number 20 scoop; place on jelly-roll pan; then place in freezer, covered.
2. Wash, hull, and slice strawberries; if desired, sweeten slightly; refrigerate.
3. Wash, pit, and stem 1½ cups cherries; cut in halves. Wash remaining cherries, leaving stems on. Refrigerate all.
4. Remove paper from meringue; set on serving plate.
About 15 minutes before serving:
1. Peel and slice bananas; let stand in a bit of lemon juice a few minutes, to prevent discoloration. In large bowl, combine berries, halved cherries, and banana slices.
2. Pile ice-cream balls in meringue shell; around them arrange mixed fruit. Then tuck leaves under meringue as pictured, and garnish plate with cherries with stems. Makes about 16 servings.

Ice-Cream Desserts

STRAWBERRY ALASKA

1 baked 9-inch yellow-cake layer	1 10-ounce package frozen sliced strawberries, thawed, drained
2 pints strawberry ice cream	5 egg whites, unbeaten
	10 tablespoons granulated sugar

Day before:
1. Place baked cake layer on foil-covered cardboard circle.
2. Let ice cream soften slightly; then pile in center top of cake layer; make a hollow in center top of ice cream, then fill with drained strawberries; freeze.
Next day:
1. In large bowl, with mixer at high speed, beat egg whites until frothy; gradually sprinkle in sugar, about 2 tablespoons at a time, beating until stiff peaks form when beater is raised.
2. With metal spatula spread about two thirds of this meringue mixture over top and sides of Alaska.
3. Now put remaining meringue in decorating bag with number 3 tube in place; decorate top and sides of Alaska in any pattern desired. Return to freezer for at least 1 hour.
About 20 minutes before serving:
1. Start heating oven to 500°F.
2. With 2 wide spatulas lift Alaska to cookie sheet; place in oven for about 2 or 3 minutes, or until meringue is just tinged with brown.
3. Remove from oven; with help of spatulas, place Alaska on serving plate. Let soften slightly, if necessary, then with long-bladed sharp knife cut into wedges. Makes 12 servings.

ICE-CREAM INSPIRATIONS
(Pictured on page 40)

We embellish the Great American Favorite—ice cream, what else?—with an unbelievable number of toppings and sauces. You'll want to try each and every one. Serve them at once or place in freezer until serving time.

FROSTED STRAWBERRIES: Top lemon or pineapple sherbet with sugar-frosted fresh strawberries.
MOCHA-WALNUT: Combine 1 10-ounce jar chocolate-caramel sauce with 1 tablespoon instant coffee powder, dissolved in 2 tablespoons hot water, and ½ cup chopped walnuts or pecans. Serve over vanilla ice cream.

HOT JAM: Heat favorite jam or preserves, then layer with vanilla ice cream in parfait glasses or sherbets.

CINNAMON POLKA DOT: Sprinkle tiny red cinnamon candies between layers of lemon sherbet.

CEREAL-HAT: Try a sprinkling of sugar-coated cereal on top of almost any flavor ice cream.

BING-BANG: Heat canned, pitted Bing cherries; spoon over strawberry ice cream.

SPRING PARFAIT: In each parfait glass, layer strawberry ice cream, dessert topping, sliced strawberries, vanilla ice cream, and dessert topping again; garnish with whole strawberries.

MELTED DELIGHT: Prepare 1 package regular chocolate pudding-and-pie-filling mix as package label directs. Remove from heat; lay wax paper directly on surface. Let stand at room temperature 20 minutes; remove wax paper. In parfait glasses or nappy dishes, alternate spoonfuls of warm pudding and vanilla ice cream.

SPICY PEACH: In small saucepan combine 1 1-pound 13-ounce can cling-peach slices and syrup with ½ teaspoon cinnamon. Heat; then spoon over vanilla ice cream.

HONEY-CITRUS: In small saucepan combine 1 cup liquid honey with ½ cup water and grated peel of 1 lemon and 1 orange. Boil, over medium heat, 5 minutes; cool; refrigerate until ready to serve. Spoon over lemon sherbet.

AMBROSIA ICE: Combine 1 cup canned pineapple juice with 1 cup orange juice and ¼ cup lemon juice. Pour into ice-cube tray. Prepare 1 package dessert topping mix as package label directs, using 1 teaspoon vanilla extract. Spoon it in layer on top of fruit juices. Freeze until juice is firm—about 2 hours. Cut into squares, then place in refrigerator for about 20 minutes before piling in sherbet glasses. Garnish with mint.

MINT-PINEAPPLE: Combine ¾ cup white corn syrup with 1 9-ounce can crushed pineapple, ¼ teaspoon peppermint extract, and a few drops green food color. Cover; refrigerate until thoroughly chilled. Serve over vanilla ice cream.

TART-CHERRY: Combine 1 12-ounce jar (1 cup) cherry preserves with 3 tablespoons lemon juice and 3 tablespoons water. Refrigerate until chilled. Serve with vanilla ice cream.

GRATED CHOCOLATE: Sprinkle finely grated sweetened or unsweetened chocolate over favorite ice cream.

CHOCOLATE DOTS: Dot vanilla or chocolate ice cream with chocolate candy bars cut into small pieces.

ICE-CREAM BOMBE

2 pints vanilla ice cream, slightly softened
2 pints chocolate ice cream, slightly softened
1 pint orange sherbet, slightly softened
1 pint strawberry ice cream, slightly softened

Day before, or up to 1 week ahead:
1. In chilled 2½-quart ovenglass bowl or mold, with back of spoon spread vanilla ice cream so it lines bottom and sides of bowl evenly up to 1-inch from top sides, leaving center hollow. Freeze until firm.
2. Remove from freezer; spread layer of chocolate ice cream over vanilla layer, smoothing it with back of spoon and leaving center hollow. Freeze until firm.
3. Remove bowl from freezer; fill hollowed center of chocolate ice cream with orange sherbet, packing it down firmly. Freeze until firm.
4. Spread strawberry ice cream evenly over top of firm ice-cream layers, filling bowl completely. Place wax paper over top and freeze overnight, or until needed.
About 1 hour before serving:
Remove wax paper. Carefully dip bowl into lukewarm water 5 to 10 seconds. Loosen top edge of ice cream with spatula. Unmold Ice-Cream Bombe onto wooden board or metal tray; return to freezer until serving time.
At serving time:
With help of 2 wide spatulas, remove Ice-Cream Bombe from board to chilled serving dish. Serve immediately, cut into wedges with sharp knife, dipped in warm water. Makes 12 to 16 servings.

MAHOGANY SUNDAES

1 cup granulated sugar
1½ cups hot water
2 tablespoons instant coffee powder
3 tablespoons cornstarch
2 tablespoons cold water
3 tablespoons butter or margarine
¼ cup rum
1 pint coffee ice cream
1 pint vanilla ice cream

Day before, or early on day:
1. In large skillet, over medium heat, melt sugar until golden, stirring constantly after it begins to melt.
2. Combine hot water with coffee powder. Slowly and carefully stir into melted sugar, then cook, stirring, until sugar is completely dissolved.
3. Remove sauce from heat. Mix cornstarch with cold water; stir into sauce. Continue cooking, stirring constantly, until sauce is thickened and smooth. Remove

Ice-Cream Inspirations

from heat; add butter and rum; stir until butter is melted. Refrigerate, covered, until needed.

About 5 minutes before serving:

Reheat sauce. Into each of 6 sherbet dishes spoon 1 scoop coffee ice cream and 1 scoop vanilla ice cream. Pour hot sauce over each sundae. Makes 6 servings.

CRÈME DE MENTHE CLOUD
(Pictured opposite)

3 pints lemon sherbet	15 to 18 violets and leaves
¼ cup green crème de menthe	

Day before, or earlier, if desired:

Let sherbet stand in large bowl at room temperature until slightly softened; add crème de menthe; blend well. Spoon into 6-cup tower mold, being careful to avoid making air spaces. Cover with foil or saran; freeze.

Several hours before serving:

Place small cookie sheet in freezer for a few minutes. Then invert mold on it; lay cloths, wrung out of hot water, over mold, then repeat until mold can be lifted off. Return sherbet, on sheet, to freezer.

At serving time:

With help of wide spatulas, slide sherbet to serving plate. Around base on top arrange violets and leaves as pictured. Serve at once. Makes 8 servings.

ICE CREAM CLAD IN CHOCOLATE
(Pictured opposite)

4 cups fine chocolate wafer crumbs (2 8½-ounce packages)	2 pints pistachio ice cream, slightly softened
1 cup melted butter or margarine	2 pints chocolate ice cream, slightly softened
2 pints vanilla ice cream, slightly softened	Fresh coconut or flaked coconut

Any time up to 2 weeks ahead:

1. Prepare chocolate wafer crumbs in electric blender, or by rolling wafers with rolling pin.
2. In medium bowl combine crumbs with melted butter; set aside ⅔ cup crumb mixture. Firmly press remaining crumbs over bottom and up sides of 9-inch spring-form pan, with round insert in place. Freeze about 15 minutes, or until firm.
3. Remove from freezer and quickly spread vanilla ice cream over bottom in even layer; sprinkle with ⅓ cup reserved crumbs. Freeze until firm. Repeat with pistachio ice cream and chocolate ice cream, but omit sprinkling crumbs on chocolate layer. Cover pan with foil; return to freezer until needed.

Early on serving day:

1. Place serving plate in freezer to chill.
2. Make coconut curls using pieces of fresh coconut

and vegetable parer; wrap loosely in foil; refrigerate.

About 10 minutes before serving:

1. Invert spring-form pan onto chilled serving plate. Release catch and remove sides and bottom of pan.
2. Garnish cake with coconut curls. To serve, cut into wedges with knife dipped in cold water. Freezer-wrap any leftover cake and freeze. Makes 12 servings.

COCOA-CREAM RING
(Pictured opposite)

About 3 pints vanilla ice cream	2½ cups packaged cocoa-flavor rice or corn cereal
1 4-ounce bar German's sweet cooking chocolate	Bottled chocolate-caramel sauce
1 cup broken walnuts	

1. Chill 1¼-quart ring mold in refrigerator.
2. Form 10 balls from vanilla ice cream; place on cookie sheet; freeze.
3. In double boiler, over warm, *not hot,* water, melt chocolate; add walnuts and cereal. Toss until uniformly coated with chocolate. Press lightly into chilled ring mold; refrigerate 20 to 25 minutes.
4. Unmold cereal mixture onto serving plate; heap ice-cream balls in center; drizzle with chocolate-caramel sauce. Makes 6 servings.

PEAR SUNDAE PIE

¾ cup granulated sugar	1½ cups fine graham-cracker crumbs
2 tablespoons cocoa	¼ cup light-brown sugar, packed
Salt	
Dash cinnamon	⅛ teaspoon mace
¼ cup white corn syrup	1 quart vanilla ice cream
¾ cup milk	1 1-pound 14-ounce can pear halves, drained
Butter or margarine	¼ cup chopped walnuts
½ teaspoon vanilla extract	

Early on day:

1. Make sauce: In small saucepan blend granulated sugar, cocoa, ¼ teaspoon salt, and cinnamon well. Stir in corn syrup, milk, and 2 tablespoons butter. Boil 10 minutes; remove from heat; add vanilla; refrigerate.
2. Start heating oven to 350°F.
3. Blend graham-cracker crumbs with brown sugar, ⅓ cup melted butter, mace, and ¼ teaspoon salt. With back of spoon, press to bottom and sides of 9-inch pie plate, not on rim.
4. Bake 10 to 12 minutes, or until light brown; cool.
5. Turn ice cream; slightly softened, if necessary, into bowl; through it, in marbled effect, swirl ¼ cup chilled chocolate sauce. Then quickly spoon ice cream into chilled pie shell; freeze until firm.

Just before serving:

Arrange pear halves, cut side down, on ice cream.

Crème de Menthe Cloud

Cocoa-Cream Ring

Ice Cream Clad in Chocolate

Melon Crescents à la Mode

Oranges Supreme

Drizzle with chocolate sauce; sprinkle with nuts. Serve in wedges; pass rest of sauce. Makes 8 servings.

MELON CRESCENTS À LA MODE
(Pictured opposite)

Toppings:
Pecan halves
Marshmallow cream
Orange marmalade
Apricot preserves

For each serving:
¼ small ripe cantaloupe
2 canned-pineapple slices
2 medium balls vanilla ice cream
1 medium ball orange sherbet

About 1 hour ahead:
1. Chop 3 or 4 pecan halves for each serving; place in small bowl. Spoon some of other toppings into small bowls; arrange all on tray with serving spoons.
2. Pare, then cut into 4 equal lengthwise strips, one-fourth of cantaloupe. Lay these slices along lengthwise center of dessert or banana-split dish.
3. Drain pineapple slices well; cut each slice in half, then place 2 halves across front and 2 halves across back of cantaloupe as pictured; refrigerate.
Just before serving:
Place ice cream and sherbet on melon as pictured. Serve at once; pass toppings. Delicious!

ORANGES SUPREME
(Pictured opposite)

6 large oranges
1 cup sliced pitted dates
1 cup drained, canned cling-peach slices, cut up
1 cup sliced, drained maraschino cherries
1 cup drained, canned crushed pineapple
3 tablespoons brandy (optional)
4 pints vanilla ice cream or orange sherbet

Any time up to 2 weeks ahead:
1. With sharp knife cut each orange into "petals" about two thirds down sides; with fingers pull pulp away from peel, leaving a shell. If necessary cut thin slice from bottom of each shell so it stands erect. (Refrigerate orange pulp for later use as fruit cocktail.)
2. In bowl combine dates, peaches, cherries, pineapple, and brandy.
3. Now, with tablespoon, pack some of ice cream or sherbet into bottom of one shell; pour in about ⅓ cup fruit mixture. Pack shell with more ice cream, then press "petals" upright into ice cream to keep orange shape; top with a little more fruit mixture. Immediately place on tray in freezer; repeat.
4. When oranges are frozen, wrap each in foil or saran; store in freezer until needed.
About 15 to 20 minutes before serving:
Unwrap oranges; let stand at room temperature 15 to 20 minutes, or until soft enough to eat. Makes 6 servings.

Soufflés

HOT APPLE SOUFFLÉ

½ cup butter or margarine
½ cup regular all-purpose flour
2 cups cold milk
⅛ teaspoon salt
6 tablespoons granulated sugar
Grated peel of ½ lemon
2 medium apples
4 eggs, separated
2 tablespoons slivered toasted almonds
Confectioners' sugar
Light cream

About 2 hours and 15 minutes before serving:
1. In medium saucepan melt butter; stir in flour, then milk. Cook, stirring constantly, until smooth and thickened. Blend in salt, sugar, and lemon peel; let cool slightly, stirring occasionally.
2. Start heating oven to 325°F.
3. Meanwhile, wash, pare, then cut each apple into about 10 lengthwise wedges; remove core and seeds from each wedge. Arrange evenly over bottom of casserole which measures 8 cups to brim.
4. Beat egg whites until stiff. Blend egg yolks into flour-milk mixture, then carefully fold in egg whites. Pour over apples; sprinkle with almonds.
5. Bake 1 hour and 15 minutes, or until light brown and firm.
6. Sprinkle with confectioners' sugar and serve *at once* along with light cream. Makes about 6 servings.

HOT CHOCOLATE SOUFFLÉ

1 package regular chocolate-, or chocolate-fudge-, pudding-and-pie-filling mix
Dash salt
1¼ cups milk
3 egg yolks
1 teaspoon vanilla extract
3 egg whites
½ cup heavy cream, or soft vanilla ice cream (optional)

About 1 hour and 20 minutes before serving:
1. Start heating oven to 350°F. Grease 1-quart baking dish or 5-cup soufflé dish.
2. In medium saucepan combine pudding mix, salt, and milk; cook, stirring constantly, over medium heat, until mixture is just boiling; then remove from heat.
3. In medium bowl, with mixer at high speed, beat egg yolks until light and thick; then beat them into hot pudding until smooth; beat in vanilla.
4. In large bowl, with mixer at high speed, beat egg whites until soft peaks form; then carefully fold in pudding mixture. Pour into prepared baking dish; set in pan of hot water.

5. Bake 1 hour.

6. Serve *at once*, topping each serving with whipped cream or soft vanilla ice cream, if desired. Makes 6 servings.

HOT COCONUT SOUFFLÉ
(Pictured below)

Butter or margarine
½ cup quick-cooking tapioca
⅓ cup granulated sugar
2 cups milk
3 eggs, separated
1 3½-ounce can flaked coconut

¾ teaspoon lemon extract
¼ teaspoon salt
3 tablespoons flaked coconut
Whipped cream, flavored with sherry or rum

About 1 hour before serving:

1. Start heating oven to 350°F.

2. Cut a 28-inch length of foil, 6 inches wide. Wrap foil around outside of china soufflé dish which measures 5 cups to brim, so foil stands 3 inches above rim. Tie tightly with string. Butter inside of foil collar, but do not butter dish.

3. In double boiler combine tapioca and sugar; add milk, then cook, over boiling water, about 10 minutes, or until thick, stirring occasionally.

4. Meanwhile, beat egg yolks until thick and light color. Wash beater to remove all traces of yolks.

5. Remove tapioca mixture from heat; stir in 2 tablespoons butter, can of coconut, and lemon extract.

6. Beat egg whites until foamy; add salt and beat until stiff but not dry.

7. Lightly fold egg yolks into coconut mixture until just blended; turn into large bowl; fold in egg whites until just blended. Turn into prepared dish; sprinkle with 3 tablespoons coconut.

8. Bake 45 minutes.

9. Carefully run small spatula between soufflé and foil,

Hot Coconut Soufflé

snip string, and remove collar. Serve *immediately* with whipped cream. Makes 6 servings.

HOT SOUFFLÉ GRAND MARNIER

3 egg whites	¾ cup milk
Butter or margarine	2 egg yolks, beaten
Granulated sugar	⅛ teaspoon cream of tartar
2½ tablespoons regular all-purpose flour	Grand Marnier
	Whipped cream
Dash salt	

1. In medium bowl, let egg whites stand to come to room temperature—about 1 hour.
2. Start heating oven to 450°F. Butter well, then sprinkle with sugar, 1-quart soufflé dish or casserole.
3. In saucepan melt 2 tablespoons butter; remove from heat. Stir in flour, salt, and milk; cook, stirring, over medium heat, until thickened and smooth. Stir in 3 tablespoons sugar; cool slightly; add egg yolks.
4. In medium bowl, beat egg whites until foamy; add cream of tartar, beating until stiff peaks form when beater is raised. Into egg whites, gently fold egg yolk mixture and 3 tablespoons Grand Marnier. Turn into prepared dish. Set in 1 inch hot water in pan.
5. Bake 10 minutes, then turn oven heat down to 325°F. and bake 15 minutes longer.
6. Serve at once, with whipped cream and more Grand Marnier to pour over. Makes 2 or 3 servings.

OMELET SOUFFLÉ

Granulated sugar	Strawberry jam
5 egg whites	Pour cream (optional)
4 egg yolks	

About 30 minutes before serving:
1. Start heating oven to 400°F. Generously grease 17½-inch ovenproof platter, or 1½-quart oval skillet, or 10-by-6-by-2-inch glass baking dish; sprinkle with 1 teaspoon sugar.
2. In large bowl, with mixer at high speed, beat egg whites until stiff and shiny, but still moist. Over them gradually sprinkle 3 tablespoons sugar, beating until sugar is dissolved and egg whites form peaks when beater is raised.
3. Next, in small bowl, with mixer at same speed, beat egg yolks until thick and lemon-colored, adding 1 or 2 tablespoons sugar, depending on sweetness desired. Lightly, but completely, fold egg yolks into egg whites. Spoon mixture onto prepared platter, mounding it around sides, with a depression in center.
4. Bake 18 to 20 minutes, or until puffed and well tinged with brown. Remove from oven at once; sprinkle with a bit of sugar.
5. Spoon jam into center; serve *at once,* with pour cream, if desired. Makes 4 to 6 servings.

COLD SOUFFLÉ GRAND MARNIER
(Pictured on page 48)

¾ cup granulated sugar	½ cup glacéed mixed fruits, drained
1 cup water	
Grand Marnier	¾ cup canned roasted diced almonds
2 tablespoons lemon juice	
1 envelope plus 2 teaspoons unflavored gelatin	2½ cups heavy cream
	¼ teaspoon salt
7 eggs, separated	2 preserved kumquats, cut in 4 wedges

Day before:
1. In medium saucepan combine ½ cup sugar, water, ½ cup Grand Marnier, lemon juice, gelatin, and egg yolks, stirring until smooth. Cook, over low to medium heat, stirring, until mixture coats spoon and gelatin is dissolved. Pour into large bowl; refrigerate until like unbeaten egg white.
2. Meanwhile, soak finely-cut-up glacéed fruits in 2 tablespoons Grand Marnier. Prepare foil collar for soufflé dish which measures 7½ cups to brim, as in step 4 of Marble Bavarian Soufflé, page 50. Lightly butter inside of foil collar.
3. Into cooled gelatin mixture fold ½ cup almonds and glacéed fruits.
4. Whip 2 cups cream. Beat egg whites with salt until soft peaks form; then gradually add ¼ cup sugar, beating until stiff. Fold cream and egg whites into gelatin mixture. Pour into prepared soufflé dish; refrigerate overnight.
About 20 minutes before serving:
1. Sprinkle ¼ cup almonds around top of soufflé. Carefully remove foil collar.
2. Whip ½ cup cream until stiff. Use in decorating bag with number 6 tube in place, to press out a continuous circle of e's, clockwise, next to inner edge of almonds. Center with large rosette. Dot kumquats over whipped cream as pictured. Makes 10 servings.
FOR 5 OR 6: Make half above recipe, using 4 eggs and 1 envelope gelatin, in 3-cup serving dish with foil collar, or 6-cup serving dish, omitting collar.

COLD COFFEE SOUFFLÉ
(Pictured on page 48)

3 cups strong coffee beverage	½ teaspoon salt
	1 teaspoon vanilla extract
1 cup milk	1¼ cups heavy cream
3 envelopes unflavored gelatin	1½ teaspoons confectioners' sugar
6 eggs, separated	Grated peel of 2 oranges
Granulated sugar	

Day before, or early on day:
1. In double-boiler top combine coffee, milk, and gelatin; scald, stirring occasionally to dissolve gelatin.

2. In small bowl, with mixer at medium speed, beat egg yolks with 2 tablespoons granulated sugar and salt until light and lemon-colored.

3. With mixer at low speed, gradually add some of coffee mixture to egg yolks, blending well. Then, pour this mixture into rest of hot coffee mixture in double-boiler top, stirring. Cook, over very hot, *not boiling*, water, stirring constantly, until mixture thickens slightly and coats spoon. Pour into large bowl; refrigerate, stirring occasionally, until mixture mounds when dropped from spoon—about 1½ to 2 hours.

4. Meanwhile, prepare foil collar for soufflé dish which measures 6 cups to brim, as in step 4 of Marble Bavarian Soufflé, page 50.

5. Now beat egg whites until frothy; then gradually add 1 cup granulated sugar and vanilla, beating until stiff. Fold into gelatin mixture and beat smooth.

6. Whip 1 cup heavy cream; fold into gelatin mixture. Pour into prepared soufflé dish; refrigerate until set, or overnight.

At serving time:

1. Carefully remove foil collar.

2. Whip ¼ cup cream with confectioners' sugar until stiff. Use in decorating bag with number 2 tube in place, to press out small rosettes around top outer edge of soufflé; then press out desired design on top center of soufflé.

3. Now gently pat orange peel around sides of soufflé and sprinkle some on top as pictured. Makes 10 to 12 servings.

COLD RASPBERRY-CREAM SOUFFLÉ
(Pictured here)

4 10-ounce packages frozen raspberries, slightly thawed	3 envelopes plus 2 teaspoons unflavored gelatin
Granulated sugar	¼ cup water
2 tablespoons lemon juice	7 egg whites*
	¼ teaspoon salt
	4 cups heavy cream

Day before, or early on day:

1. Prepare foil collar for soufflé dish which measures 7½ cups to brim, as in step 4 of Marble Bavarian Soufflé, page 50.

2. In medium saucepan, slightly crush all but 9 or 10 raspberries with fork. (Wrap reserved berries in foil and return to freezer for later use.) To rest of berries add ¼ cup sugar, lemon juice, and 3 envelopes gelatin. Stir over medium heat until gelatin is dissolved.

3. Chill over ice cubes, stirring constantly, until mixture *just* mounds when dropped from spoon; remove to 3-quart bowl at once. Sprinkle 2 tablespoons gelatin on water; dissolve over hot water.

4. Meanwhile, in large bowl beat egg whites with salt

Orange Soufflé Brûlée, Cold Coffee Soufflé, Cold Soufflé Grand Marnier,
Cold Raspberry-Cream Soufflé, Marble Bavarian Soufflé

until soft peaks form; then gradually add ¼ cup sugar, beating until stiff. In another large bowl combine heavy cream, gelatin and 2 tablespoons sugar; beat until stiff.

5. Into chilled raspberry mixture fold egg whites and half of whipped cream. Refrigerate 1 cup whipped cream. Spoon some of raspberry mixture into prepared soufflé dish, even with rim. Spread with half of remaining whipped cream; next, half of remaining raspberry mixture; repeat. Refrigerate 1 hour.

6. Now put refrigerated whipped cream in decorating bag with number 6 tube in place. Carefully remove foil collar. Press out 4 evenly spaced "commas" from top edge to center of soufflé. Press out one rosette in center, one between every two "commas." Refrigerate.

Just before serving:

Arrange reserved raspberries as pictured on page 48. Makes about 16 generous servings.

*Use egg yolks in custard or eggnog sauce, bread pudding, etc.

ORANGE SOUFFLÉ BRÛLÉE
(Pictured on page 48)

1 cup orange juice	1 3-ounce package lady-
Sherry	fingers, in large pieces
¾ cup granulated sugar	1 cup cut-up orange
1 tablespoon grated lemon	sections
peel	2 cups heavy cream
3 tablespoons lemon juice	¼ teaspoon salt
1 envelope plus 2	3 tablespoons light-brown
teaspoons unflavored	sugar
gelatin	About 15 whole blanched
7 eggs, separated	almonds

Day before:

1. In medium saucepan combine orange juice, ½ cup sherry, ½ cup granulated sugar, 1 teaspoon lemon peel, lemon juice, gelatin, and egg yolks; stir until smooth. Cook, over medium to low heat, stirring until mixture coats spoon and gelatin is dissolved. Pour into large bowl; refrigerate until cool and consistency of unbeaten egg white.

2. In small bowl place ladyfinger pieces; over them pour ⅓ cup sherry and let soak a few minutes. Meanwhile, prepare foil collar for soufflé dish which measures 7 cups to brim, as in step 4 of Marble Bavarian Soufflé, below.

3. Into cooled orange mixture fold ladyfingers and orange sections. Whip cream until stiff. Beat egg whites with ¼ teaspoon salt until soft peaks form, then gradually add ¼ cup granulated sugar, beating until stiff. Into orange mixture fold whipped cream and egg whites; turn into prepared soufflé dish; refrigerate.

Early on day:

1. Preheat broiler 15 minutes (it has to be very hot). Meanwhile, sprinkle brown sugar over top of soufflé;

insert almonds here and there. Brown quickly, close to high heat, 30 seconds. Refrigerate until chilled.

2. Before serving, remove foil collar. Then gently pat 2 teaspoons lemon peel around sides of soufflé. Makes about 10 servings.

Note: Leftovers keep well, refrigerated for a few days.

FOR 5: Halve above ingredients, but use 4 eggs and 2½ teaspoons gelatin, the same amount of brown sugar and almonds; use 6-cup ovenproof casserole, omitting foil collar.

MARBLE BAVARIAN SOUFFLÉ
(Pictured on page 48)

3 envelopes unflavored	1 quart milk
gelatin	4 squares semisweet choco-
1 cup cold water	late
8 eggs, separated	4 tablespoons cocoa
1 cup granulated sugar	About 6 drops yellow food
1 tablespoon vanilla	color
extract	2 cups heavy cream
¼ cup regular all-purpose	¼ teaspoon salt
flour	

Day before, or early on day:

1. Sprinkle gelatin over water to soften.

2. In large saucepan combine egg yolks with ¾ cup sugar and vanilla; blend in flour, stirring until smooth; now add milk, blending well. Cook, over low to medium heat, stirring constantly, until custard coats back of spoon. Remove from heat.

3. Add gelatin mixture, stirring until completely dissolved. Refrigerate, stirring occasionally, until mixture mounds when dropped from spoon.

4. Meanwhile, fold 35-inch piece of foil (12 inches wide) in half lengthwise; wrap around outside of soufflé dish which measures 10 cups to brim, so collar 3-inches high stands above rim; fasten with cellophane tape.

5. Melt chocolate in small saucepan over hot, *not boiling,* water. Divide cooled custard mixture in half, placing each half in large bowl. Into one half, stir chocolate and cocoa until smooth. Into other half stir food color.

6. Whip cream. Beat egg whites with salt until soft peaks form; gradually add ¼ cup sugar, beating until stiff. Into chocolate mixture fold half of egg whites and half of whipped cream. Into yellow mixture fold rest of cream and egg whites.

7. Into soufflé dish alternately spoon yellow and chocolate mixtures. Then, with rubber spatula, cut through mixture several times, swirling to make marbleized effect. Refrigerate several hours or overnight.

Just before serving:

Carefully remove foil collar. Makes about 16 servings.

FOR 6 TO 8: Make half above recipe, using 5-cup china soufflé dish with foil collar, or 8-cup glass serving dish, omitting collar.

Gelatin Desserts

COCONUT CREAM

1 cup milk	2 cups heavy cream,
1 envelope unflavored	whipped
gelatin	1 tablespoon vanilla extract
¼ cup cold water	⅓ to ½ cup flaked
½ cup granulated sugar	coconut
⅛ teaspoon salt	Chocolate sauce (from jar)
	Caramel sauce (from jar)

Day before:

1. Scald milk. Meanwhile, sprinkle gelatin on water to soften. To scalded milk add gelatin, sugar, and salt; stir until dissolved. Refrigerate until slightly thickened, stirring occasionally.
2. Fold in whipped cream, vanilla, and coconut. Turn into 1½-quart mold; refrigerate.

About 1 hour before serving:

1. Dip coconut mold into hot water for a minute or two to loosen. Invert serving plate on mold; then invert both; lift off mold. Refrigerate until served.
2. At serving time, drizzle chocolate sauce in spiral design over Coconut Cream; then drizzle on caramel sauce in same way. Makes 8 servings.

APPLE SNOW

1 envelope unflavored	¼ teaspoon salt
gelatin	Snipped crystallized ginger
¼ cup cold water	2 egg whites
2 cups canned applesauce	8 ivy leaves
½ cup granulated sugar	Custard Sauce, below
1½ teaspoons lemon juice	(optional)

Day before:

1. Sprinkle gelatin over cold water to soften.
2. In large saucepan combine applesauce, sugar, lemon juice, salt, and 2 tablespoons ginger. Over low heat bring to simmer; remove from heat; add gelatin and stir until dissolved.
3. In large bowl beat egg whites until very stiff (reserve yolks for Custard Sauce); then fold in hot applesauce mixture. (Mixture will appear curdled.)
4. Rinse 1½-quart bowl with cold water; pour in applesauce mixture; refrigerate. Make Custard Sauce.

Next day, just before serving:

1. Dip bowl of Apple Snow in hot water, part way up, for a minute or two to loosen; invert serving dish on bowl, then invert both; lift off bowl.
2. Garnish Apple Snow with ivy leaves and small clus-

ters crystallized ginger (about ¼ cup in all). Serve with Custard Sauce. Makes 8 servings.

CUSTARD SAUCE: In double-boiler top heat 1 cup milk until tiny bubbles appear around edge. In medium bowl beat 2 egg yolks; stir in 1½ tablespoons granulated sugar and ⅛ teaspoon salt. Slowly add hot milk, stirring constantly to avoid cooked egg specks. Return mixture to double boiler; cook, over hot, *not boiling,* water, stirring constantly, until thick enough to coat back of spoon. Pour at once into bowl; cool; add ½ teaspoon vanilla; lay wax paper on surface; refrigerate.

APRICOT CREAM, TIFFANY
(Pictured on page 52)

1 8¾-ounce can unpeeled	4 egg whites, at room
apricot halves, drained	temperature
2 1-pound 14-ounce cans	2 tablespoons granulated
unpeeled apricot halves,	sugar
drained	1 tablespoon vanilla extract
2 to 4 tablespoons brandy	1 cup heavy cream,
1 envelope unflavored	whipped
gelatin	Ladyfingers
¼ cup cold water	Grated peel of 1 lemon
	Green grapes (optional)

Day before, or 4 hours before serving:

1. Select 9 to 12 firm apricot halves; refrigerate.
2. In large saucepan simmer remaining apricot halves with brandy, *stirring constantly,* until they come to a slow boil—about 5 minutes. Then purée in food mill or strainer; refrigerate.

About 2 hours and 30 minutes before serving:

1. Sprinkle gelatin on water to soften; stir over boiling water until completely dissolved and clear; cool.
2. In small bowl, with mixer at high speed, beat egg whites until frothy; then gradually add sugar, beating until stiff peaks form.
3. Now, in large bowl combine apricot purée, gelatin mixture, and vanilla. Carefully fold in egg-white mixture until no large pieces remain; then fold in whipped cream.
4. Fill 2-quart glass dessert bowl two-thirds full of apricot mixture. Now line sides of bowl with ladyfingers, pressing ends slightly into dessert to hold them upright.

Cherry-Ruby Goblet, Creamy Ambrosia, Baked Apples à la Suisse

Minted Limelight Parfait

Apricot Cream, Tiffany

Finish filling bowl with apricot cream, straightening ladyfingers, if necessary. Sprinkle with lemon peel. Refrigerate 2 hours, or until cold.

At serving time:
Arrange reserved apricot halves in ring on top of apricot cream as pictured, placing small bunch of grapes in center, if desired. Makes 8 to 10 servings.

TOASTED SNOW SQUARES

1 envelope unflavored gelatin	1 tablespoon grated lemon peel
1 cup granulated sugar	2 tablespoons lemon juice
1¼ cups boiling water	⅓ cup heavy cream, whipped
3 egg whites, unbeaten	1 cup graham-cracker crumbs (about 16 crackers)
¼ teaspoon salt	
1 teaspoon vanilla extract	
2 egg yolks	
⅓ cup melted butter or margarine	

Several hours ahead:
1. In medium bowl blend gelatin with ⅔ cup sugar. Add boiling water, stirring until dissolved; let cool.
2. In large bowl place egg whites, salt, and vanilla; add gelatin mixture. Then, with mixer at high speed, beat until consistency of thick cream. Turn into 9-by-9-by-2-inch cake pan. Refrigerate until firm.

About 1 hour before serving:
Make butter sauce: Beat egg yolks until thick and lemon-colored. Gradually add ⅓ cup sugar, beating continually. Now blend in melted butter, lemon peel and juice. Fold in whipped cream; refrigerate.

At serving time:
Cut gelatin mixture into 1-inch squares; roll each square in crumbs. Heap in sherbet glasses; then top with butter sauce. Makes 8 to 10 servings.

FRUITED PASTEL CHEESE RING

3 envelopes unflavored gelatin	¾ cup creamed cottage cheese
2 cups cold water	1 unpared red apple, thinly sliced
¼ cup maraschino-cherry juice	1 unpared green pear, thinly sliced
¼ cup lemon juice	2 tablespoons lemon juice
Red food color	3 large oranges, sectioned
¾ cup commercial sour cream	10 maraschino cherries
1 cup (8 ounces) finely-crumbled Roquefort cheese	

About 4 hours before serving:
1. Sprinkle gelatin on cold water to soften; then heat, in small saucepan, stirring constantly, until gelatin is dissolved. Stir in cherry juice, ¼ cup lemon juice, and enough food color to make deep pink; refrigerate until cool.
2. Meanwhile, in large bowl, with mixer at medium speed, beat together sour cream and Roquefort and cottage cheeses until lumps are very small. Into this mixture gradually beat gelatin mixture; turn into 5½-cup ring mold; refrigerate until set.

About 15 minutes before serving:
1. Combine apple and pear slices with 2 tablespoons lemon juice; add orange sections.
2. Unmold cheese ring onto serving plate; fill center with mixed fruits. Top with maraschino cherries, drained and dried on paper towels. Makes 8 servings.

CHERRY-RUBY GOBLET
(Pictured opposite)

1 1-pound 1-ounce can pitted Bing cherries	2 cups boiling water
½ cup port or Marsala wine	Cold water, if needed
2 3-ounce packages cherry-flavor gelatin	1 pint soft vanilla ice cream

Early on day before:
1. Drain cherries, refrigerating juice. In small bowl, having steep sides, place drained cherries; cover with wine. Refrigerate, uncovered, 3 hours.
2. In large bowl dissolve gelatin in boiling water. Drain cherries, reserving wine; combine with reserved cherry juice and enough cold water to measure 1½ cups; stir into gelatin mixture. Pour mixture into 12-by-8-by-2-inch baking pan or jelly-roll pan. Refrigerate 20 to 25 minutes, or until slightly thickened.
3. Arrange cherries in rows in gelatin; refrigerate.
4. When firm, cut dessert into cubes, with one cherry in each. Heap, lightly, in 6 or 8 sherbet glasses. Refrigerate until needed.

At serving time:
Top cherry mixture in each glass with large spoonful of ice cream; pass rest as sauce. Makes 6 to 8 servings.

LEMON-ORANGE FOAM
(Pictured on page 61)

2 teaspoons unflavored gelatin	2½ tablespoons lemon juice
½ cup cold water	Grated peel of ½ lemon
4 eggs, separated	1 large unpeeled orange
¼ cup granulated sugar	

Day before, or early on day:
1. Sprinkle gelatin on cold water to soften.
2. In small bowl, with mixer at medium speed, beat egg yolks with sugar until foamy — about 5 minutes; gradually add lemon juice, then peel, blending well.
3. Turn egg-yolk mixture into double-boiler top, then stir in gelatin. Cook, over boiling water, stirring con-

stantly, until mixture coats back of spoon. Then turn into medium bowl and refrigerate until slightly thickened, stirring occasionally.

4. Beat egg whites until they hold shape; gently fold into lemon-gelatin mixture. Spoon into 6 sherbet glasses; refrigerate until needed.

About 10 minutes before serving:

Cut orange into thin slices, then cut each slice in half. Arrange half slices, rounded side up, around inside edge of sherbet glasses. Now halve 3 of half slices; then place one, point end up, on top center of each glass as pictured. Makes 6 servings.

MINTED LIMELIGHT PARFAIT
(Pictured on page 52)

2 3-ounce packages lime-flavor gelatin	1 package dessert-topping mix
2 cups boiling water	3 tablespoons white crème de cacao
1 cup cold water	¼ cup milk
9 tablespoons green crème de menthe	

Early on day:

1. Stir gelatin into boiling water until dissolved. Stir in cold water and 6 tablespoons crème de menthe. Pour into shallow pan; refrigerate until firm.
2. In small bowl, with mixer at high speed, combine dessert topping mix with 3 tablespoons crème de menthe and the crème de cacao, beating until smooth. Gradually add milk, beating until topping holds shape—about 8 minutes (don't overbeat). Cover; refrigerate.

Just before serving:

1. Force firm gelatin mixture through chilled ricer. (The gelatin will sparkle and glitter.)
2. Layer gelatin with spoonfuls of dessert topping in parfait glasses. Decorate each with a rosette of topping; pass remaining topping. Makes 5 or 6 servings.

MOCHA FROTH
(Pictured on page 61)

1 envelope unflavored gelatin	1 tablespoon cocoa
⅓ to ½ cup granulated sugar	⅛ teaspoon salt
1 tablespoon instant coffee powder	1½ cups boiling water
	1 teaspoon vanilla extract
	2 egg whites
	Dessert topping (optional)

Early on day:

1. In medium bowl mix thoroughly gelatin, sugar, coffee powder, cocoa, and salt. Add boiling water, stirring until gelatin and cocoa are completely dissolved. Add vanilla; refrigerate until slightly thicker than unbeaten egg white.
2. Add egg whites; with mixer at high speed, beat until light coffee color. Refrigerate until firm.

At serving time:

Spoon gelatin mixture into 6 to 8 dessert dishes, placing each spoonful bottom up, so any clear mocha gelatin is on top. Serve with dessert topping, if desired. Makes 6 to 8 servings.

MANDARIN ORANGES IN A CLOUD
(Pictured on page 61)

1 envelope unflavored gelatin	3 cups milk
Granulated sugar	1 teaspoon grated lemon peel
¼ teaspoon salt	1 cup drained canned Mandarin oranges
3 eggs, separated	

Day before:

1. In double-boiler top mix gelatin, ¼ cup sugar, and salt. Stir in egg yolks, then slowly stir in milk. Cook, over boiling water, stirring constantly, until mixture coats back of spoon. Remove from heat; stir in lemon peel.
2. In large bowl beat egg whites until moist peaks form; gradually beat in ¼ cup sugar, beating until stiff. Now fold in hot gelatin mixture; refrigerate.

Next day, just before serving:

Spoon some of gelatin mixture into each of 6 sherbet glasses; add a few orange sections; top with more of gelatin mixture. Top each with 1 or 2 orange sections. Makes 6 servings.

PEACHES WITH CUSTARD CUBES
(Pictured on page 61)

1 envelope unflavored gelatin	1 cup milk
⅓ cup nonfat dry milk powder	3 eggs
3 tablespoons granulated sugar	¼ teaspoon salt
1 cup cold water	1 teaspoon almond extract
	½ teaspoon nutmeg
	1 cup drained canned cling-peach slices

Day before, or early on day:

1. In double-boiler top combine gelatin, dry milk, and sugar. Slowly add some of cold water, stirring until completely smooth; then slowly stir in remaining water and milk.
2. Meanwhile, in small bowl beat eggs with salt until well blended. Now beat in some of milk mixture; then stir this into milk mixture in double boiler, being careful so froth does not form on top. Cook, stirring constantly, over hot, *not boiling*, water, until mixture coats back of spoon. *Immediately* remove from heat. Stir in almond extract and nutmeg; pour into 9-by-5-by-3-inch loaf pan; refrigerate until set. Refrigerate peaches, covered.

About 15 minutes before serving:

With sharp knife, cut custard into 1-inch squares. Spoon some into each of 6 sherbet dishes; top with a few peach slices; rest of custard squares, then garnish with mint sprigs, if desired. Makes 6 servings.

PINEAPPLE-SNOW PUDDING

3½ cups canned pineapple
   juice
3 envelopes unflavored
   gelatin
6 tablespoons granulated
   sugar
⅛ teaspoon salt
2 teaspoons grated lemon
   peel

¼ cup lemon juice
1½ cups heavy cream
1½ cups flaked coconut
4 cups halved fresh strawberries, or 2 10-ounce
   packages frozen straw-
   berries, thawed
4 canned pineapple slices,
   quartered

Day before, or early on day:

1. Into 1 cup pineapple juice, in small bowl, stir gelatin and sugar; let stand 5 minutes. Set bowl in boiling water; stir until gelatin is dissolved.
2. In large bowl combine 2½ cups pineapple juice, salt, lemon peel and juice; stir in gelatin mixture. Refrigerate until like unbeaten egg white.
3. With mixer at high speed, beat gelatin mixture until fluffy. Whip cream; quickly fold whipped cream and ¾ cup coconut into gelatin. Pour into 2-quart mold; refrigerate until set.

Just before serving:

Unmold pudding onto large serving plate; sprinkle top with some coconut and strawberries; arrange some of quartered pineapple, strawberries, and rest of coconut around base. Pass rest of pineapple and strawberries. Makes 8 servings.

TANGERINE RICE MOLD

½ cup uncooked regular
   or processed white rice
Cold water
1½ cups milk
½ teaspoon salt
6 tablespoons granulated
   sugar
¾ cup milk
4 egg yolks
¼ cup granulated sugar
2 envelopes unflavored
   gelatin

3 tablespoons grated
   orange peel
2 teaspoons vanilla extract
⅓ cup canned slivered
   toasted almonds
Tangerine-Rum Sauce,
   below
2 cups heavy cream
¼ cup rum
Few tangerine or canned
   Mandarin-orange sections

Early on day:

1. Pour rice into medium saucepan; barely cover with cold water. Simmer, covered, 5 minutes; drain. Add 1½ cups milk, salt, and 6 tablespoons sugar. Simmer, covered, stirring occasionally, 15 minutes, or until rice is very tender. Set aside.
2. In double boiler, combine ¾ cup milk, egg yolks, and ¼ cup sugar. Cook over hot, *not boiling*, water, stirring often, until smooth, thickened custard.

3. Meanwhile, sprinkle gelatin over ⅓ cup cold water to soften. Stir into custard mixture; then cook, stirring until gelatin is dissolved. Remove from hot water; stir in orange peel and vanilla. Now stir in rice and almonds. Refrigerate 1 hour and 30 minutes, or until mixture begins to set, stirring often.
4. Meanwhile, make Tangerine-Rum Sauce.
5. Whip cream with rum. When rice mixture begins to set, fold in whipped cream. Pour into lightly-oiled 2-quart mold. Refrigerate until set—about 2½ hours.

At serving time:

Quickly dip mold almost to rim, in and out of hot water; invert serving dish over mold; invert both; lift off mold. Garnish with tangerine sections; pass sauce. Makes 8 to 10 servings.

TANGERINE-RUM SAUCE: In small saucepan combine 1 cup reconstituted frozen or canned tangerine juice, 3 tablespoons granulated sugar, and 1 tablespoon cornstarch. Stir smooth; then bring to boil, stirring. Remove from heat; stir in 2 tablespoons rum. Refrigerate until needed.

SHIMMERING FRUIT FANTASY
(Pictured on page 56)

2 6-ounce packages orange-
   pineapple-flavor gelatin
Boiling water
1 1-pint bottle lemon-flavor
   sparkling water
1⅓ cups Chablis or
   sauterne
Ice cubes

4 or 5 canned, thawed
   frozen, or thin fresh
   peach slices
Seedless green grapes
1½ 8-ounce packages
   cream cheese, at room
   temperature
6 tablespoons milk
¼ teaspoon nutmeg
Dash cinnamon

Early on day before:

1. Have ready a 2-quart china soufflé dish, or dish of same capacity having flat bottom and straight sides.
2. In bowl place 1 package gelatin. Pour 1½ cups boiling water over it, then stir until gelatin is completely dissolved. Now stir in sparkling water and ⅔ cup Chablis until blended.
3. Partially fill large bowl with ice cubes; in it set bowl

Shimmering Fruit Fantasy

Fruit Mosaic

of gelatin; stir gelatin constantly until some of it just mounds when dropped from spoon. Remove from ice; pour 2 cups gelatin mixture into soufflé dish (leave rest of it in bowl at room temperature). In gelatin mixture in soufflé dish arrange peach slices and ⅓ cup grapes in pattern pictured.

4. Now carefully spoon rest of gelatin mixture over fruit, making sure top is smooth and level. Refrigerate until almost firm—about 40 minutes.

5. With fork, beat cream cheese with milk, nutmeg, and cinnamon until mixture is very smooth. Spoon this cheeese mixture over gelatin, using small spatula to make even layer; clean sides of dish; refrigerate.

6. Now make up second package of gelatin as in steps 2 and 3 above; when it mounds, carefully spoon over cheese layer; refrigerate until serving time next day.

Just before serving:

Lower soufflé dish into hot water up to ½ inch of top for 1 to 2 minutes. Run long spatula all around, being sure it goes all the way to bottom of dish to completely loosen gelatin. Invert serving plate on top of soufflé dish; invert both, then shake gently until gelatin slips out. Garnish with tiny bunches of grapes as pictured. Makes 8 servings.

FRUIT MOSAIC
(Pictured opposite)

Orange slices	Blackberries
Strawberries	2 envelopes unflavored
Honeydew-melon balls	gelatin
Plum slices	1 cup cold water
Orange sections	⅔ cup granulated sugar
Lime wedges	¼ teaspoon salt
Cherries	2 cups boiling water
Cantaloupe balls	½ cup lemon juice
Grapes	

Early on day:

1. With picture as guide, arrange fresh fruits on a shallow 16-inch glass platter: In center on top of an orange slice and around a large strawberry, alternate honeydew-melon balls with plum slices. Surround with a ring of orange sections and lime wedges, then rows of cherries, strawberries, honeydew and cantaloupe balls, and grapes, in that order. Now border mosaic with halved orange slices that have had all but center bit of pulp cut away; place strawberry halves inside, then finish with row of blackberries. Refrigerate.

2. In large bowl soften gelatin in cold water; add sugar, salt, and boiling water; stir until dissolved. Add lemon juice. Refrigerate until like unbeaten egg white.

3. Pour gelatin mixture over fruits, coating well, and being careful not to disturb design. Refrigerate until set. Cut into wedges; serve with pie server. Makes 12 servings.

Fruit Desserts

BAKED APPLES À LA SUISSE
(Pictured on page 52)

6 baking apples	1 1¾-ounce jar red
⅓ cup chopped walnuts	cinnamon candies
⅓ cup seedless raisins	30 whole blanched almonds
⅓ cup granulated sugar	3 preserved kumquats
1½ cups water	6 glacéed cherries
	Cream

Day before:

1. Wash and core apples. Then, with small pointed knife, divide each apple into 8 lengthwise wedges (petals), cutting them only halfway down from top.

2. Mix walnuts with raisins, then use some to fill center of each apple. Place, side by side, in shallow baking dish.

3. In small saucepan combine sugar, water, and cinnamon candies. Bring to boil, stirring constantly; let simmer 5 minutes. Pour this syrup over apples; let cool slightly; cover with saran and refrigerate.

About 1 hour and 30 minutes before serving:

1. Start heating oven to 350°F.

2. Bake apples about 1 hour, or until fork-tender, spooning syrup over them occasionally while they bake.

3. Meanwhile, split 24 almonds in half lengthwise. Halve kumquats, then scoop out insides. Cut a slit in top of each glacéed cherry. Set a cherry in center of each kumquat.

4. When apples are done, place filled kumquat on center of each. Now arrange an almond half on top of each apple petal as pictured, with its point under kumquat. Serve warm, or cold with whipped or pour cream. Makes 6 servings.

BETTY-STYLE APPLES

1½ cups fresh bread	¼ teaspoon nutmeg
crumbs	¼ teaspoon cinnamon
¼ cup melted butter or	2 teaspoons grated lemon
margarine	peel
3 medium apples	1½ teaspoons lemon juice
⅓ cup brown sugar	3 tablespoons water

About 1 hour and 20 minutes before serving:

1. Start heating oven to 350°F.

2. Toss bread crumbs with butter. Wash, pare, core, and thinly slice apples.

3. Combine brown sugar, nutmeg, cinnamon, and lemon peel. In 1-quart casserole arrange one third of

crumbs. Top with half of apples, half of sugar mixture, half of remaining crumbs, then rest of apples and sugar. Spoon on lemon juice mixed with water. Then top with rest of crumbs.

4. Bake 1 hour, or until apples are done. Serve with vanilla ice cream, if desired. Makes 3 or 4 servings.

APPLES AMERICANA

12 small McIntosh apples	1 stick whole cinnamon
1 cup granulated sugar	Confectioners' sugar
2 cups water	

Make any time up to 2 hours before serving:

1. Wash apples. In medium, heavy-gauge saucepan, bring granulated sugar, water, and cinnamon stick to boil. Add apples, a few at a time; boil until they are fork-tender, *but still shapely*—about 3 to 5 minutes. Remove from syrup, one at a time.

2. In heated compote, filled with a cushion of crumpled foil, or on heated platter, arrange apples in a pyramid, having 7 apples on bottom tier, with 1 in center, 4 in second tier, and 1 on top.

3. Now boil syrup to 234°F. on candy thermometer. Then pour it over apples in a *very thin* coating; lightly sift confectioners' sugar over all.

4. To serve, allow 1 apple apiece. Makes 12 servings.

RED CHERRY RING

2 1-pound cans pitted red sour cherries	1/4 teaspoon salt
Red food color	4 1/2 cups packaged biscuit mix
1 1/2 cups granulated sugar	1 pint heavy cream
3 tablespoons cornstarch	1/4 teaspoon almond extract
1 1/2 tablespoons butter or margarine	

About 2 hours and 30 minutes before serving:

1. Start heating oven to 375°F. Generously grease 3-quart ring mold.

2. Thoroughly drain cherries, reserving juice. To cherries add food color to brighten red. To reserved cherry juice add enough water to measure 2 1/4 cups liquid; brighten with food color.

3. In saucepan pour cherry juice over mixture of sugar, cornstarch, and butter; cook until thickened and clear; add salt; pour into prepared ring mold.

4. Prepare biscuit-mix dough as package label directs for biscuits; then, on floured surface, roll dough to 1/4 inch thickness. Cover with drained cherries. Roll up as for jelly roll; cut into 12 even slices. Lay in ring mold, cut side down.

5. Bake 1 hour; invert onto serving plate; cool.

6. Whip cream with almond extract. Mound in center of cooled cherry ring. Or serve cherry ring warm, without cream. Makes 12 servings.

QUILE
(Glorified Ambrosia)

3 cups orange juice	3 3-ounce packages ladyfingers
1/4 cup lemon juice	
1 cup granulated sugar	2 cups grated fresh coconut, or 1 4-ounce can flaked coconut
1 1-pound can crushed pineapple, lightly drained	
1 8-ounce can pineapple tidbits, drained	Candied cherries (optional) Candied citron (optional)

Day before:

1. In saucepan combine orange juice, lemon juice, and sugar. Cook, uncovered, 10 minutes, or until consistency of maple syrup. Pour over crushed pineapple and pineapple tidbits.

2. In 2 1/2-quart serving dish alternate layers of ladyfingers, pineapple mixture, and coconut, ending with coconut. Garnish with cherries and citron, if desired. Refrigerate until serving time next day. Makes 12 to 16 servings.

GRAPEFRUIT MERINGUE
(Pictured on page 61)

2 medium grapefruit	1/4 teaspoon salt
3 egg whites	1/4 cup granulated sugar

About 30 minutes before serving:

1. Start heating oven to 375°F.

2. Cut grapefruit in half; snip center core from each half, then cut around all sections; arrange halves in shallow baking dish.

3. In small bowl beat egg whites with salt until stiff enough to hold shape; gradually add sugar, beating until stiff. Pile some of meringue mixture on top of each grapefruit half.

4. Bake 15 minutes. Makes 4 servings.

ORANGE RICE CREAM

1 cup uncooked regular white rice	2 cups heavy cream
	1/2 teaspoon vanilla extract
6 oranges	1 tablespoon semisweet chocolate pieces
4 to 6 tablespoons granulated sugar	

Make early on day, or 1 hour before serving:

1. Cook rice as package label directs; refrigerate.

2. Peel oranges; cut into sections; reserve 10 sections for garnish. Cut rest in half; sprinkle with sugar; refrigerate.

3. Just before serving, whip cream until stiff; add vanilla. Fold in rice and halved orange sections (if very juicy, drain off some of juice). Arrange in serving dish; garnish with reserved orange sections and chocolate pieces. Makes 6 to 8 servings.

PEACH-BUTTERSCOTCH CRISP

1 1-pound 13-ounce can
 cling-peach slices,
 drained
½ cup brown sugar, packed
½ cup regular all-purpose
 flour
¼ teaspoon salt
¼ teaspoon cinnamon
¼ cup butter or margarine
Vanilla ice cream

About 30 minutes before serving:
1. Start heating oven to 425°F.
2. Arrange peach slices in 9-inch pie plate.
3. In medium bowl combine sugar, flour, salt, and cinnamon. With fork or pastry blender, cut in butter until crumbly. Sprinkle this mixture in thick layer over peaches.
4. Bake 20 minutes, or until top is golden and crisp. Serve warm, topped with ice cream. Makes 6 servings.

PEARS SUPREME

16 canned pear halves,
 drained
About ½ cup Dutch-process
 cocoa
1 egg
1 cup confectioners' sugar
2 tablespoons melted butter
 or margarine
1 teaspoon vanilla extract
1 cup heavy cream
Semisweet-chocolate square

Day before:
Place pear halves, rounded side down, in 12-by-8-by-2-inch baking dish. Spoon 2 teaspoons to 1 tablespoon cocoa down center of each pear half. Cover with remaining pear halves, rounded side up; secure each with toothpick. Cover; refrigerate.
Several hours before serving:
1. Beat egg; beat in confectioners' sugar, butter, and vanilla. Whip cream until stiff; fold into egg mixture. Cover; refrigerate.
2. Make a few chocolate curls by carefully paring thin slices from warm chocolate square with vegetable parer; set aside.
At serving time:
Remove picks from pears; arrange pears in compote or serving dish. Pour on sauce; garnish with chocolate curls. Makes 8 servings.

PEARS ARMENONVILLE
(Pictured on page 2)

1 cup granulated sugar
¼ cup lemon juice
2 tablespoons butter or
 margarine
2 cups boiling water
8 ripe pears
2 10-ounce packages frozen
 raspberries, thawed
¼ cup port wine
Commercial sour cream

Day before:
1. In saucepan simmer sugar, lemon juice, butter, and water 5 minutes.
2. Start heating oven to 350°F.
3. Pare pears, leaving stems on; arrange in 3-quart casserole; pour on lemon mixture.
4. Bake, covered, about 45 minutes, or until tender; cool right in liquid, then drain.
5. Sieve raspberries; put purée in large bowl or 12-by-8-by-2-inch baking dish; stir in wine. Lay pears in this mixture; refrigerate, turning pears occasionally and spooning sauce over them to keep color even.
At serving time:
Serve chilled pears with sauce in nappy dishes; pass sour cream to spoon over them. Makes 8 servings.

FRUIT QUARTET

1 13½-ounce can pineapple
 tidbits
1 16-ounce can grapefruit
 sections
1 11-ounce can Mandarin-
 orange sections
1 16- or 17-ounce can
 cling-peach slices
1 cup miniature marsh-
 mallows
1 cup commercial sour
 cream
½ cup flaked coconut

About 2 hours before serving:
1. Drain all fruits well (refrigerate syrups for later use).
2. In medium bowl combine fruits, marshmallows, sour cream, and coconut; refrigerate.
3. At serving time heap in nappy dishes or sherbet glasses. Makes 6 servings.

CREAMY AMBROSIA
(Pictured on page 52)

1 cup heavy cream
½ cup commercial sour
 cream
1 3½-ounce can flaked
 coconut
1 cup miniature marsh-
 mallows
2 cups orange sections
1½ cups grapefruit
 sections
Maraschino cherries
 (optional)

Day before:
1. In medium bowl whip cream until stiff. Fold in sour cream, coconut, and marshmallows.
2. Prepare orange and grapefruit sections; set some of

each aside for layering and top garnish; cut up rest; fold into cream mixture; cover and refrigerate.

Just before serving:

Spoon cream mixture into serving glasses, layering and topping with reserved orange and grapefruit sections. Top each with maraschino cherry, if desired. Makes 6 to 8 servings.

STRAWBERRY-MELON MEDLEY
(Pictured opposite)

1 10-ounce package frozen sliced strawberries, thawed	2 tablespoons granulated sugar
Water	Red food color
½ stick cinnamon	2 cups fresh strawberries, quartered
1 teaspoon grated lemon peel	2 cups honeydew-melon balls
3 tablespoons cornstarch	

Day before, or early on day:

1. In saucepan combine thawed strawberries, 1½ cups water, cinnamon, and lemon peel; bring to boil, then simmer 5 minutes; press through fine sieve.
2. Return strawberry purée to saucepan; blend cornstarch, ¼ cup cold water, and sugar; then stir into purée. Bring to boil, stirring constantly, then simmer 1 minute. Add few drops food color to tint deep red. Then pour into bowl; place piece of wax paper on surface; let cool, then refrigerate.

About 15 minutes before serving:

Remove wax paper. Beat purée with hand beater until fluffy. Fold in strawberries and melon balls, reserving a few of each for garnish. Spoon into 6 parfait glasses; top with reserved strawberries and melon balls.

CREAMY FRUIT DELIGHT
(Pictured opposite)

1 10-ounce package frozen sliced strawberries, thawed	3 tablespoons cornstarch
	Red food color
Water	1 1½-ounce package vanilla rennet-custard dessert
½ stick cinnamon	
1 teaspoon grated lemon peel	1 cup fresh strawberries, quartered

Day before, or early on day:

1. In saucepan combine thawed strawberries, 1½ cups water, cinnamon, and lemon peel; bring to boil, then simmer 5 minutes; press through fine sieve.
2. Return strawberry purée to saucepan; blend cornstarch with ¼ cup cold water; stir into purée. Bring to boil, then simmer 1 minute, stirring constantly. Add few drops food color. Pour into bowl; lay piece of wax paper directly on surface of purée; let cool, then refrigerate.

3. Prepare rennet-custard dessert as package label directs, pouring into bowl; refrigerate.

About 15 minutes before serving:

1. Beat purée with hand beater until fluffy; stir in fresh strawberries, reserving some for garnish.
2. In 6 parfait glasses carefully layer spoonfuls of strawberry purée and rennet-custard dessert, starting and ending with purée. Garnish top with reserved strawberries; serve at once. Makes 6 servings.

FOUR FRUIT COMPOTE

1 large orange	3 tablespoons lemon juice
1 small cantaloupe	¼ cup granulated sugar
½ pound seedless grapes	¼ teaspoon mace
3 ripe pears	2 tablespoons rum

Several hours before serving:

1. Grate peel from orange, reserve; then cut off remaining peel. Cut orange into segments, free membrane, dropping segments into large bowl.
2. Cut cantaloupe into wedges, 2 inches wide; seed, then pare. Cut wedges into large cubes; add to oranges with stemmed grapes.
3. Pare pears, quarter, cut out cores, then cut into large cubes. Sprinkle pears with lemon juice; add to fruit mixture.
4. In saucepan simmer ½ cup water with reserved grated orange peel, sugar, and mace until sugar is dissolved. Pour hot over fruits; add rum, if desired. Cover; refrigerate until served. Makes 6 to 8 servings.

HOT FRUIT COMPOTE ALAMODE

2 3⅓-ounce cans flaked coconut	1 1-pound 4-ounce can pineapple spears
3 to 4 pints vanilla ice cream	2 tablespoons lemon juice
	¾ teaspoon nutmeg
2 1-pound 13-ounce cans purple plums	¼ cup liquid honey
1 1-pound 13-ounce can unpeeled whole apricots	1 tablespoon salad oil

Several hours before serving:

1. Toast half of coconut in 325°F. oven 10 minutes, stirring occasionally; cool.
2. Form ice cream into balls; roll half in toasted coconut, rest in plain coconut; freeze.

About 15 minutes before serving:

1. Drain plums, apricots, and pineapple. Arrange plums in center of 10- or 12-inch skillet. Arrange apricots on one side of plums, pineapple on other side. Sprinkle with lemon juice, then nutmeg. Drizzle with mixture of honey and salad oil.
2. Heat until compote is warm, occasionally spooning over it any syrup that seeps from fruit. Serve hot over ice-cream balls. Makes 10 to 12 servings.

Lemon-Orange Foam, Mocha Froth, Mandarin Oranges
in a Cloud, Grapefruit Meringue, Peaches with Custard Cubes,
Strawberry-Melon Medley, Creamy Fruit Delight

Desserts for Dieters

STRAWBERRY-GLAZED ORANGE-CHEESE PIE
(low-calorie and low-fat)

½ cup packaged cornflake crumbs (or crumbs from 1¾ cups cornflakes)
1 tablespoon melted butter or margarine
Salt
Granulated sugar
1 8-ounce container creamed cottage cheese
1 envelope plus 1 teaspoon unflavored gelatin
1 cup orange juice
1 teaspoon grated lemon peel
2 tablespoons lemon juice
3 egg whites
½ cup strawberry or raspberry jam or preserves
Few drops red food color (optional)

1. Start heating oven to 375°F.
2. In 9-inch pie plate thoroughly mix crumbs, melted butter, pinch salt, and 1 tablespoon sugar. With spoon, press mixture evenly around bottom and up sides of pie plate.
3. Bake 8 to 10 minutes; cool.
4. Meanwhile, press cottage cheese through fine sieve.
5. In medium saucepan mix 1 envelope gelatin, ¼ cup sugar, orange juice, lemon peel, and lemon juice; let stand 5 minutes to soften gelatin.
6. Heat mixture, over low heat, until gelatin is dissolved; add cottage cheese, then beat with hand beater until smooth. Refrigerate until slightly thicker than unbeaten egg white.
7. Beat egg whites and ¼ teaspoon salt until soft peaks form; gradually add ¼ cup sugar, 1 tablespoon at a time, beating until stiff peaks form. Fold gelatin mixture into egg whites; turn into cooled pie shell; refrigerate until set—about 1 hour.
8. Meanwhile prepare strawberry glaze: In small saucepan mix 1 teaspoon gelatin, jam, and enough food color to make bright red; let stand 5 minutes to soften gelatin. Bring mixture to rolling boil; cool; refrigerate until consistency of thick white sauce.
9. Pour glaze over pie, then with spatula, gently spread mixture to edge of pie; refrigerate at least 2 more hours before serving. Makes 10 servings. (*150 calories per serving; 1 gram fat per serving*)

CHERRY-GLAZED PINEAPPLE-CHEESE PIE: Prepare and bake pie shell as above; make filling, substituting 1 cup canned pineapple juice for orange juice. While pie is setting, make cherry glaze: In small saucepan mix 1 tablespoon cornstarch with 2 tablespoons granulated sugar; slowly stir in ½ cup liquid drained from canned, pitted sour cherries. Simmer, stirring constantly, until clear and thickened. Add 1 cup very thoroughly drained canned, pitted red sour cherries, 1 tablespoon lemon juice, ¼ teaspoon almond extract, and few drops red food color; cool to room temperature. Use to glaze pie; chill at least 2 hours. Makes 10 servings. (*150 calories per serving*)

McINTOSH MERINGUE
(low-calorie)

1 egg white
Granulated sugar
Dash ground ginger
2 8-ounce cans or
1 1-pound can unsweetened applesauce

Early on day, or up to 1 hour before serving:
1. Start heating oven to 425°F.
2. In small bowl beat egg white until soft peaks form; gradually add 4 teaspoons sugar, 1 teaspoon at a time, and ginger, beating until smooth, stiff, glossy peaks form.
3. Into applesauce stir 2 tablespoons sugar; divide applesauce among 4 6-ounce custard cups; top each with dollop of meringue mixture.
4. Bake 4 to 6 minutes, or until nicely browned. Serve warm, or refrigerate and serve cold. Makes 4 servings. (*90 calories per serving*)

GRAPE ICE CREAM
(low-calorie, low-fat, and low-sodium)

¼ cup cornstarch
1 cup granulated sugar
Dash cinnamon
Dash nutmeg
1½ cups bottled grape juice
1 teaspoon vanilla extract
½ cup water
2 or 3 tablespoons lemon juice
1 14½-ounce can skimmed evaporated milk,* undiluted

Day before, or early on day:
1. In medium saucepan thoroughly mix cornstarch, sugar, cinnamon, and nutmeg. Stir in a little grape juice to form smooth paste; then add remaining grape juice, vanilla, water, and lemon juice. Cook, stirring constantly, until mixture boils and thickens. Cool, then refrigerate, stirring occasionally, until well chilled.
2. While grape mixture is chilling, place evaporated milk in large bowl; place milk and mixer beaters in freezer until ice crystals form ½ to 1 inch in from edge of bowl.
3. When grape mixture is chilled and ice crystals have formed (if milk is frozen solid, stir and let thaw slightly), with mixer at high speed, beat milk until consistency

of whipped cream. Slowly drizzle grape mixture over whipped milk, beating constantly. Beat until smooth, scraping bowl and beaters as needed.

4. Freeze right in bowl or other container until hard. Makes about 2 quarts or 12 servings. (*120 calories per serving*)

*If skimmed evaporated milk is not available, use regular whole evaporated milk. (*150 calories per serving*)

GRAPEFRUIT BRÛLÉE
(low-calorie)

2 medium grapefruit	⅛ teaspoon cinnamon
4 teaspoons granulated sugar	4 maraschino cherries

About 20 minutes before serving:
1. Preheat broiler 10 minutes, or as manufacturer directs.
2. Meanwhile, halve grapefruit; with knife, cut around each section. Mix together sugar and cinnamon; sprinkle evenly over grapefruit halves.
3. Broil 5 minutes, or until warm and bubbly; top each half with a maraschino cherry. Makes 4 servings. (*90 calories per serving*)

HOMEMADE PINEAPPLE SHERBET
(low-calorie and low-fat)

1 1-pound 4-ounce can crushed pineapple, undrained	½ teaspoon vanilla extract
	2 tablespoons lemon juice
1 envelope unflavored gelatin	Dash salt
	2 cups cold skim milk or reliquefied nonfat dry milk
¼ cup granulated sugar	
1 teaspoon grated lemon peel	

About 5 to 6 hours before serving:
1. If sherbet is to be frozen in freezer compartment of refrigerator, turn refrigerator control to coldest setting. Select medium bowl that will fit into freezer or freezer compartment.
2. Drain pineapple, reserving 1 cup syrup. In small saucepan sprinkle gelatin over pineapple syrup; let stand 5 minutes to soften. Heat, stirring constantly, until gelatin is dissolved—do not boil. Stir in sugar, lemon peel, vanilla, lemon juice, and salt until dissolved.
3. Place milk in the medium bowl, then slowly stir in gelatin mixture. (Mixture may appear curdled.) Freeze, stirring every 30 minutes or so, until ice crystals have formed throughout most of mixture, but it is not firm.
4. With mixer or hand beater, beat until smooth. Fold in drained pineapple. Return to freezer; freeze until firm enough to spoon out. (Reset refrigerator to normal temperature, if necessary.) If sherbet freezes too hard, let stand at room temperature for up to 30 minutes to

soften slightly. Makes 8 servings. (*150 calories per serving and negligible fat*)

PEACH PUDDING MELBA
(low-calorie and low-fat)

1 1-pound can freestone-peach halves	1 teaspoon vanilla extract
	½ cup canned skimmed evaporated milk
2 tablespoons cornstarch	
½ cup orange juice	⅓ cup currant, raspberry, or strawberry jam or jelly, melted
1 tablespoon lemon juice	
Dash cinnamon	

Early on day:
1. Drain peaches, reserving syrup. In medium saucepan slowly stir ½ cup reserved syrup into cornstarch to form smooth paste. Then stir in orange juice, lemon juice, cinnamon, and vanilla until smooth. Cook, stirring constantly, until thickened. Let cool to room temperature; then refrigerate, stirring occasionally, until cold and firm.
2. In freezer, in deep, medium bowl, chill evaporated milk and mixer beaters until crystals form around sides of bowl.

After ice crystals have formed, at least 1 hour before serving:
With mixer at high speed, beat evaporated milk until consistency of whipped cream. To it add chilled orange pudding, beating until smooth. Evenly divide among 6 nappy or dessert dishes; top each with peach half, smooth side up. Pour on jam or jelly; refrigerate until serving time. Makes 6 servings. (*135 calories per serving*)

FRUITED FLOATING ISLAND
(low-calorie)

1 1-pound can peeled apricots, drained	1 1-pound can cling-peach slices, drained
1 1-pound can applesauce	3 egg whites, unbeaten
¼ teaspoon cinnamon	⅓ cup granulated sugar
Dash nutmeg	¼ teaspoon vanilla extract
2 tablespoons lemon juice	

At least 20 minutes before serving:
1. Start heating oven to 450°F.
2. Halve apricots and remove pits.
3. In 9-inch layer-cake pan, mix together applesauce, cinnamon, nutmeg, lemon juice, apricots, and peaches.
4. In medium bowl, beat egg whites until soft peaks form. Then add sugar, a small amount at a time, beating constantly, until mixture forms stiff peaks. Beat in vanilla. Drop this meringue, by large spoonfuls, in 8 separate dollops, on top of fruit.
5. Bake 4 to 7 minutes, or until lightly browned. Serve warm or cold. Makes 8 servings. (*140 calories per serving*)